VALUE GIVE

Become The Person With The Midas touch Who
Handles Things & Make Them Valuable

OLADIMEJI OLUTIMEHIN

VALUE GIVER:
Become The Person With The Midas touch Who Handles
Things & Make Them Valuable

Millionaire Maker Publishers
A Imprint of First Millionaire Maker Nig Ltd
8 Afunbiowo Street, Old Garage
P.O Box 2465
Akure, Ondo State
Nigeria

+2349071602727
1stmillionairemakernng@gmail.com

Printed in Nigeria.

Dedication
For Jim Rohn.
Through whom I learned that to give value is the best investment in my future. Thank you Jim.

Table Of Content

INTRODUCTION

I n 2000, as a fresh graduate from the university, I took up a job in a business that was just starting. My salary was only N500 but I was excited to be working. But there was some-one who had no degree, who was earning 14 times what I was earning. Instead of being angry, I asked myself what he was doing that was earning him that kind of income. He must be doing something that was important for him to earn more than me.

The answer wasn't really shocking but it was educative. He was just 14 times more valuable to our employer than I was. He was the one who was bringing in 80% of the revenue. From then on I began to seek to understand what it means to be more valuable. The quest to be a value giver started even though I had no name for it.

Instead of using the money I earned to buy clothes, I used them to buy books to read and learn. My father had taught me that my value is in what I know. So I sought to know more through books. I read and learned from a particular authors' book that my income is directly proportional to my contribution. And to contribute more, I will need to learn more.

From then on, I seek to bring more to the table than I was paid. Everywhere I worked, I learn about what is important to the employer and then give more than is expected. As a consequence, I got my salary increased every month. I implemented this concept somewhere and it made me a consultant earning 6 figure income and then 7 figure income.

Thats when I knew I have found a pearl with a great price. It's the secret that many people have been looking for all their lives and have never found. The secret is the same as that of the law of sowing and reaping: my compensation is equivalent to the value I contributed. I refused to use my money for anything but to keep increasing my value.

One day I was with a man who I have studied for 20 years, Bishop David Oyedepo. And he told me that they will never buy another jet again, rather people will but it for them. I wondered how that will happen. As if he was reading my thoughts, he answered, that by impacting them with great value. He says, "*The quality of your spiritual impact is what determines the material returns that attend to you.*"

From then on I knew that if I can just contribute in value the equivalent of what I want to have, I will eventually have it if I don't grow weary and give up on contributions value. It's a great lesson for me and I put it to work.

I started the year 2015 with no income but with the understanding that when I add value to people, I will get compensated for it. By the end of that year, I was being compensated for the value I have given to the tune of 6 figure income monthly. Its amazing but it works.

It has worked for me as an employee and as an employer. Now I am bring out this secret and sharing it to the world. We all can be value givers. The world will be a much better place when all the 7 billion people on earth can just begin to contribute value wherever they are. That is my goal with this concept, to get 7 billion people to understand that they can get all their needs met if they can contribute the equivalent value.

The goal of this book is to show you how you can be a person who continually give value to people wherever you are. This is the one secret that Jesus Christ taught the world. He was generous with value. He gave till He gave His life for the good of people. I studied Him from when I was a kid of 10 till I was 16. He became my mentor and I wanted to be like Him. He gave value to the world.

He said, *"It is more blessed to give than to receive."* This also made me study other people who have contributed immense value to the earth and made our world better. Value Givers like John D. Rockefeller, Thomas Edison, Henry Ford, Mother Theresa, Elon Musk, Steve Jobs, Richard Branson, Oprah Winfrey and so on made our world a better place by giving value that its unique to them.

Value You Give Determines What You Get
What you give in value determines what you receive. When you keep giving value, men will give back to you in good measure, pressed down, shaken together and running over as an equivalent of the value you gave. You have to first give value if you want anything in return.
Value is a spiritual substance. When someone gives value to you, you will share your material things with them. That's why you are paying for this book. If you find the book valuable, you will also buy it for others (and we expect you to do that).

The world needs value givers, people who will never relent in creating and giving value. A tree doesn't produce fruit because of what it will get but rather to add value to humanity. It attracts people to it and makes life better for others. So also value givers give to move humanity forward and make life better for everyone.

We are in a world where only the generous create wealth. Creating and giving value to the world is the rent we are meant to pay for being on earth. If you are not giving value where you are then you are not suppose to be there. Your presence should count and should make the place where you are better.

People who take from others can also become rich but only those who continually create value create wealth. A nation is poor when it has more value takers than value givers. Values takers only take from what is available, as such consuming and even destroying the source of the value. Value givers on the other hand are always working to create new wealth. They bring about expansion in the economy of every nation they are in.

When you have more people creating and contributing value to a nation, the economy of that nation will keep expanding and life for people will get better.

The Value Giver System

This book is for people who are involved in creating and contributing value and those who are not but are desirous to be value creators and givers. The following are principles of the Value Giver which inform all that is in this book:

- **Create Unique Value.** You do have to create value that is unique to you to become a value giver. Copying the value someone has already created is not what value givers do. The value must be unique to you as you are unique. The value you create should be after your kind and not someone else's. It should carry your fingerprint and signature.

- **Connect to the Flow of the Universe.** There is a place from where creativity flows from and value givers are connected to this flow. They make themselves available for the universe to flow its goodness through them to humanity. I believe that values like the iPhone, Electric Cars, Facebook and other products that are revolutionizing our world came out of that flow. You get into the flow through growth.

- **Care for Others.** Caring for others shows that you are really connected to the flow. The flow is filled with liquid love and anyone who does things because of their love for people really shows that the flow is flowing through them. You will only be able to create value for people when you care for them. Then and only then will you produce things that will help them and make life better for them.

- **Serve With Humility.** It's not enough to create value, you have to be willing to serve people with it. Service is the rent you pay for being on the earth. Serving people with value in a humble way is the pathway to great service. Humble people listen to others and don't over estimate their own importance. Humble servants are those who know their strength and weakness and know their need for others.

- **Detach from Things.** You have to be free in order to create and give value to people. If you are not detached from the value you create, you will never want to give it away and when you get feedback, you will want to defend it rather than take the feedback and improve the value. Detachment is the state where nothing owns you. You can freely give what you value to meet the needs of others. Only in the stillness of detachment can the soul connect to the flow and create value for people.

- **Secure In Potential.** The security of value givers is in their ability to create and give value. As such, they are able to empower others to operate in their area of strength in order to complement theirs. To create massive value, you will need the cooperation of others and also empower them to operate from their area of strength. Only people who are secured can work with others to create value.

- **Invest In Growth.** No one can unleash his or her potential to create value without first growing or expanding his or her capacity. The only limitation you will ever encounter to creation of value is going to be your potential. You need to make sure that you are constantly investing in the increase of your capacity. To increase your capacity, all you have to do is to expand your mind. Your capacity is like rubber band and only become useful in the creation of value when stretched. You need to continually stretch your capacity if not it will shrink.

- **Always Exceed Expectations.** Go beyond what people expect and you will guarantee that they will always desire to receive value from you. It is the investment you make today in the future that you desire. To do that, you have to first know what it is that people are really expecting, then you can create and give more than people expect to receive. A normal performance is mediocrity and people don't just accept mediocrity. Always deliberately do for people what they don't expect to be done.
- **Take Responsibility for Outcome.** Understanding that the creation of value is based on the law of cause-and-effect. You need to know the particular cause that will create the kind of effect that you desire in people. Your value will only be acceptable to people based on the research you have done about their needs. To have a better response from people about the value you created, you will have to know the exact thing to do and create that they will like and accept.
- **Give What You Created.** There is no way you can give to anyone what you have not created. If you have not created value, then you are simply there to take and when you have taken without any creation, you exhaust the value and destroy your ability to create value. You cannot give to people what you don't have.

Why People Are Value Takers
Why is it that everywhere you go, people prefer to take value rather than create and give?

Takers are people who take value that has already been created. They are consumers of value and hardly get involved in the creation of value. Here are some reasons why people are takers.
The first reason is the focus on self. When people only care about themselves and never about others, they tend to think that the whole world revolve around them. If they are not getting any-

thing, then nothing is working. We are all tempted to always look out for what we can get. As the number of people who are selfish increases, the economy of nations will continue to shrink.

The second reason is to form a reality that revolves around them. When all you see is your world and everything you do resolves around that world, you will never venture out to know exactly what is happening to others. Its your world after all and all other people are just pawns in your hands. You are the king. This always result in the victim mentality.

The third reason is that most people don't believe they have the ability to create value, as such they give a lot of excuses that they have nothing to give. Of course, no one can ever give what they don't have. What you believe drives your behavior and actions. Most people don't believe they have what it takes to create value for people. So they stay with taking value.

The fourth reason is that they don't see value in themselves. You have to see value in yourself to be able to create value for people. If you don't see value in yourself, you will never see value in other people. And it will be hard for anyone to invest in themselves if they don't really see value in themselves. You have to see value in yourself, to invest in your growth. The more you grow, the more the value you create.

The fifth reason is that most people think that life is measured by what they possess or have accumulated. When you think life is all about what you accumulate, you become a taker instead of a giver of value. Life is measured by what you create and give to people that makes life better for them.

Most people think that their major work is just to consume what others have created already. They think the process of creating value as boring, waste of time and uninspiring, whereas in truth it is flexible and exciting. If you are not creating value each day, the time, passion, energy and resources you bring to your work is wasted. You can- and must - do better with your time. This book is about how to become a Value Giver- a person who creates and give value no matter where he or as he is.

Difference Between Value Givers & Value Takers

1. Value Takers feel they are entitle, while value Givers believe they are responsible.

2. Value Takers avoid problems, while Value Givers Embrace problems and find solutions to them.

3. Takers do what is expected, but Value Givers do much more than is expected.

4. Value Takers try to gain more than they contribute, while value Givers try to contribute more than they take.

5. Value Takers consumes the value that has been created, while Value Givers keeps creating more value than they consume.

6. Value Takers assume they know what people need, while Value Givers take time to know what people really need.

7. Value Takers are focused on themselves, while value givers are focused on others.

Century of Givers

Every society needs people who will focus on creating value. Silicon Valley is one such society that all activities happening there are focused on creating value and giving it to the world. As long as there are humans, there will always be need to create new value because problems will always exist. Solving problems for people in order to make life better for them is what value creation is all about.

This book attempts to start a movement globally where people will change their mindset from being consumers and destroyers of values to creators and contributors of value. We are in a century where the generous will win. You have the ability to create value that the world needs. It is a challenge for you to do something great with the opportunity you have to make life better for people. The Value Giver movement seeks to inspire people who long to make a difference in this world to understand what it will take to change the world and make it a better place for humanity.

CHAPTER ONE

BECOME A PERSON OF VALUE

"Try not to become a person of success, rather a man of value." Albert Einstein.

❖ ❖ ❖

If you value yourself, you will invest in yourself to become a better person. If you value people, you will develop yourself to become more valuable. You will only attract value when you are a person of value. This reminds me of the story of the founding of Stanford University.

A lady in a faded gingham dress and her husband, dressed in a homespun threadbare suit, stepped off the train in Boston, and walked timidly without an appointment into the outer office of the president of Harvard University. They had just lost their son who had attended Harvard University.

Their aim for the visit was to find a way to immortalize their son. After being ignored by the secretary and waiting for hours to see the president, they persisted. Eventually out of frustration, the president finally agreed to meet with them.

When they finally went into his office. The lady told him, "We had a son that attended Harvard for one year. He loved Harvard. He was happy here. But a year ago, he was accidentally killed. And my husband and I would like to erect a memorial to him, somewhere on campus."

The president wasn't touched, he was shocked. "madam," he said gruffly, "we can't put up a statue for every person who attended Harvard and died. If we did, this place would look like a cemetery."

"Oh, no," the lady explained quickly, "We don't want to erect a statue. We thought we would like to give a building to Harvard."

The president rolled his eyes. He glanced at the couple, and then exclaimed, "A building! Do you have any earthly idea how much a building cost? We have over seven and a half million dollars in the physical plant at Harvard."

For a moment the lady was silent. The president was pleased that he could get rid of them now.

The lady then turned to her husband and said quietly to the amazement of the president, "Is that all it costs to start a university? Why don't we just start our own?" Her husband nodded.

Mr & Mrs Leland Stanford walked out of that and travelled to Palo Alto, California where they established Stanford University, as a memorial to their son that Harvard no longer cared about.

It is instructive to know that Palo Alto today is a place where great value is created. The president was more attached to his title than to value that was why he looked down on the couple. To be a person of value, you have to be a person who cares for others and see value in them.

Success is temporal, but not value. Success is what you achieve, while value is what you do for others. Success is what you have and how you dress, but value is who you are. You have to see value in yourself to invest in yourself to be a person of value. Real success should be seen more about contributing value than just accumulating toys.

One value that Thomas Edison, John D. Rockefeller and Henry Ford created made them billionaires for life. The value still exist today. Always seek to be a person who works to create value rather than someone who wants to be successful. These men invested in themselves to become people of value.

Rockefeller's value is in Chevron, Standard Oil, Exxon Mobile and others. Edison's is in General Electric, while Henry Ford's is in Ford Motors.

My question to you then is: are you seeking to be successful and rich or you are seeking to become a person of value? When you seek to be successful and rich, they may elude you. But the best way to become successful is to become a person of value.

Becoming a person of value is not about what you wear, where you live or what you drive: these are consequence of giving value and should not be seen as value. It is about what you put into your mind and heart.

Seeking success and riches at the expense of value is placing the cart before the horse. Value is the raw material that produces success and riches.

Value is the fruit you reap after you cultivate your mind and heart. It is dependent on the seed that you sow into your heart. You have to first become a person of value before you can create value. In order to do that, you have to first invest in yourself to become valuable.

Your mind and heart are like the soil that need to be cultivated. You have to be deliberate about how you cultivate it, because it will never become valuable without an effort. Whatever you allow into it will determine who you become and what you produce. As a man thinks in his heart so is he. People who leave their mind and heart to fallow will never become valuable because weeds grow there, and weeds are never valuable.

Concept of Value

1. Value Represent Your Worth.
2. Value Determines Your Influence.
3. Value Produce Your Income.
4. Your Contribution in Life is Based on the Value you Create.
5. You Can Increase Your Value.
6. It is Robbery to Get Money When You Have not Given Value.
7. People Determine What Value Is.
8. Create Value For Whatever You Want & You Will Have It.
9. Value Can Become Obsolete Except You Keep Improving It.

For you to have a better life, then give value. But you cannot just give value without first becoming the kind of person that can really bring value to the table. Making contributions isn't magic, it is all about who you are and what you become.

Just as you cannot give what you don't have, so also you cannot create or produce anything outside who you are. You can only produce after your kind. So if you do not put in the effort to become a person of value, it will really be hard to produce what people will find valuable.

What Influences Your Value

What are the things that Affect Your Value;

1. How you see Yourself

If you see value in yourself, you will cultivate that value. Unfortunately, most people don't believe in themselves so they don't see value in themselves. Years of programming by parents and authority figures have made them not to believe they can even create any form of value.

You have to see yourself as valuable before you will do anything to ensure that you really are valuable.

People who do nothing to make themselves valuable don't because they don't see value in themselves. People prospect for oil or mineral when they think they can get the mineral from there. If you don't see value in yourself, you will never do anything to prospect for it.

If you cannot buy a $14.99 book to make yourself valuable but can buy an expensive shoe or clothe; it then means you see only value in the shoe and clothe than in yourself, then, you must think that you are worthless and can only get value from something external to you. Your value comes from within you and you have to cultivate it by investing in your growth. The more you grow, the more valuable you become.

Do you see value in yourself?

2. How You Feel About Yourself

How you feel about yourself is key to whether you do anything to add value to yourself. If you think and feel you are worthless, you will never do anything to cultivate your value. You feel you don't deserve to be better. Worthless people simply don't see themselves as valuable.

Any time you think a book is expensive, it's simply a reflection of how you feel about yourself. You will never out-invest the way you feel about yourself. If you feel you are worthless, you will never invest in becoming valuable.

I have registered for a course that is close to a million naira because I feel I am worth it. I bought books in millions last year because I believe I am worth it.

I prefer to have books to read than food because I am worth the effort. I am as valuable as that. Most people feel more valuable about their body than about their mind so they invest more in their body than in their minds.

Are you worthy?

3. What You Are Reading

What you are reading affects your value. If all you are reading and listening to is news, then you will not be valuable. What you read and listen to becomes a resources for your mind to think about. Value is either created or destroyed through your thoughts.

To become valuable I had to block people who are discussing politics on social media most especially facebook. I don't want to be reading politics but what will increase my value. I want to increase my value so I can earn $40, 000 a month. That's why I spend more on myself. I make sure that I am reading books that will increase my value to create that amount.

So read things that will increase your value. Don't seek to be known, rather seek to know and you will become known. The more you read books in the area of your strength, the better the value you can create.

What are you thinking about?

4. What Are You Thinking

What you are thinking affects your value. Reading fuels your thinking which influences your value. Growth happens when your mind gets expanded.

Most people don't even care who they are listening to or reading or who is influencing their lives. They have never made the connection between what they are thinking and the value they are bringing to the marketplace.

The person you are listening to more is affecting what you are thinking. I listened to Jim Rohn till he affected the way I am thinking.

What you are thinking is creating for you the kind of world you have. If you don't like what you are creating, then change what you are thinking. You are what you think about consistently.

You have to start noticing what you are thinking because it affects the value you create.

What are you thinking?

5. Your Willingness to Change

To become valuable you have to be willing to change. Those who never change become dinosaurs. They go into extinction and are no longer relevant.

If you are not willing to change, you will never become more valuable. To remain valuable, you have to keep changing and improving. Who you are right now is the enemy of who you can be. How valuable you are today can stop you from being valuable tomorrow. Your value never last forever.

If the world outside is changing at a faster rate than you are growing, you will soon find yourself not needed and irrelevant. You have to embrace change.

You have to give up who you are now so you can become more valuable. We all have to change in order to become more valuable. You will never grow except you first change. George Bernard Shaw said, "Progress is impossible without change, and those who cannot change their minds cannot change anything."

Are you willing to change and become more valuable than you are?

6. Your Desire to Make Life Better for People

You will never be valuable if you don't care for people. People don't care what you know if it's not going to help make their lives better. The more you are desirous of helping people become better, the more you are going to work on yourself.

Your value is based on Your ability to help people become better. For the lives of others to become better because of you, you will have to become better and more valuable. Value is in the eyes of the receiver and not the giver.

This means that you cannot just say you are valuable. People you relate with are the ones who can determine how valuable, which is based on how much you help them. So because of them you pay the price to be valuable.

Thats why I wonder why most people don't even work on themselves to become better so they can make people better. Everyone wants to earn more and become rich, but only few people are willing to work on increasing their value to people.

If you desire to make people better, you will invest in yourself to become valuable to them.

Are you helping people become better?

7. People You Associate With

Show me the people you associate with and I can predict whether you can become valuable or not. Your value is the average of that of the people you are associating with. If they are not growing their value and helping others, chances are you will be doing the same.

An enterprising, young guy came and bought my book, then called his friend to ask if he want a copy. The friend said no and told him that he takes 6 months to read a book. I told him if that guy remains his friend he will never be valuable. People you associate with influences your value.

If you have friends who are increasing their value, they will continually challenge you to increase your value. Your friends will determine what you read, where you go, who you listen to and how you see yourself.

So be sure you surround yourself with people who are working on themselves to become more valuable.

What are your friends making you do?

How To Know You Are Valuable

You Become a Go-To Person. When people keep coming to you to get ideas on what they need to do, then you are valuable. A go-to person is an expert who has the track record of getting superior results. You can be valuable by the reason of the results you produce. Make yourself valuable through your productivity and performance. Your competence will make you the go-to person.

People Talk About The Impact You Made In their Lives. When people talk about what you have done for them and how you have influenced and impacted their lives, then you are a person of value. If you want to become more valuable, serve people and do everything to make their lives better. Invest in them to succeed. Don't just help them with their career, help them also with their lives. See making their lives better as your major purpose.

People Seek Your Counsel. When people seek you out for your advice on a regular basis, it shows you have value. No one will ever seek your counsel if they don't believe that you have value to share. It's not just a perception but the fact that your advice to people have always worked. It's a sign that you are becoming valuable when people, most especially those who are better than you begin to seek you out for your counsel. Integrity and consistency will make people seek you out.

People Recommend You To Others. If people are not fevering or recommending you to others, then they don't find you valuable. When people come to you and then mentioned that someone referred them to you because of what you can do, then you are valuable. You have to keep working on yourself to always exceed the expectations of people who that they can always tell others about you.

People Pay Whatever You Ask for Your Service. You know you are valuable when whatever amount you charge for your service, people are willing to pay. For instance, people are willing to pay more for Apple products without haggling or feeling bad because they understand the value of having their products. If people still wonder why your charges are that high, you have not yet become valuable in their perception.

How to Become More Valuable

To become more valuable, you will have to work harder on yourself than you do on anything. Most employees think that if they can spend more time on the job and work harder, their employer or boss will take them as valuable. It doesn't work that way. Value is not in the time you spend working on your job, but the results you produce.

In 2013, I decided that I was going to become very valuable. So I started working harder on myself than I do on anything else as Jim Rohn counseled, *"Learn to work harder on yourself than you do on your job. If you work hard on your job you'll make a living, if you work had on yourself you can make a fortune."*

The truth is that university education was never designed to make you valuable to the marketplace. It is great no doubt. But nothing brings out the value in you like working hard on yourself. It will give you the extra that formal education will never give you. And that extra will determine a lot about your life.

Whatever you want out of life you have to give the equivalent of it in value. Whatever you want to earn or have is possible if you can just work on increasing your value.

You can earn millions of naira a month if you can increase your value to that extent. It will take time to increase your value but you will enjoy the ride. You need to be fully obsessed with increasing your value to stick to the process. Increasing your value is not an event but a process.

Here are what you need to do to increase your value;

1. Build Your Self Esteem

This is the foundation of increasing your value. It is how you feel about yourself. If you don't feel valuable, you will never add value to yourself. Self esteem is your belief about your worth and value. It heavily influences your choices and decisions.

Zig Ziglar said *"it's impossible to consistently behave in a manner inconsistent with how we see ourselves. We can do very few things in a positive way if we feel negative about ourselves."* If you feel you don't have value, you will never do anything to make yourself valuable. Everything you do will be to sabotage your value.

I used to be someone with low self esteem. I read books because I want to feel valuable. I wasn't doing it as a way to increase my value but just to prove to people I am valuable and hide how I feel about myself. I was doing things to please people.

People with low self esteem don't believe they are capable of achieving great things and becoming valuable to people, so tend to behave in such a way that they sabotage their every effort to achieve great things. You will never consistently do the things that will make you valuable if you don't believe in your worth and value.

You can never add value to yourself beyond how you see yourself. You can build your self esteem by changing what you tell yourself. Tell yourself you are amazing and greatly crafted. You have to get to the point where you have no doubt about who you are and what you can do and achieve.

Use affirmations. The more you positively affirm yourself the better you become.

2. Invest in Your Growth

The more you grow, the more valuable you become. People who are not growing and not becoming valuable. You have to find an area to grow in. Another word is to increase or expand your capacity.

People are anxious to increase their value to their employer and marketplace but are not willing to invest in their growth. As a result they stay the way they are and have their income shrink. This I believe is the reason why many people depend on their salary for as long as they are employed and return back to zero level when they eventually lose their jobs through redundancy.

There is no security in your qualification or the number of years you have served a company. Your only security is in your growth. Because if you invest in your growth and constantly grow, you will become more valuable as a person and an employee or employer. Henry Ford puts it this way, *"The only real security that a man can have in this world is a reserve of knowledge, experience and ability."*

You do that by expanding your context and increasing your context. When you expand your context, you change your mind. When you change your mind, the way you see things changes. Increasing your content is to learn more about a certain topic. Both ways are required to grow your capacity.

One involves reading books and the other thinking about what you read.

A book will not have any effect on you except you think about it. Whatever you think about, changes your mind and your perspective. When your mind changes, then you can grow.

Like a tree you have to grow, for your value to be seen. No tree bears fruit without first growing. So also no man can become valuable without growing. A tree grows to bear fruit and give it as value to people. You have to grow to produce value that people needs.

3. Develop Relevant Skills

One important skills you need to have to be valuable is problem solving skill. Your ability to solve a particular problem for a lot of people is the singular factor that will make you valuable to them. You need to know how to solve problems for people. Different problem requires different skills. All skills are learnable.

You have to develop skills for the problem you are passionate about. The intersection of your passion and your skills is where you will become more valuable.

You will not become valuable if you are trying to know how to solve all kind of problems for people. You have to develop skills to be able to solve one to three problems for them. Be known for a particular problem that only you can solve.

It takes having relevant skills to be able to meet the needs of people. To enjoy that uniqueness the problem you solve for people, you need to have a combination of skills that no one else have.

You are only as valuable as the problem you solve for people. The more skillful you are, the better and faster you can solve problems. That means you have to continually develop news skills while you improve the old ones you have.

The more skillful you are the more you do in less time and less effort you put into to creating value for people. Developing skills that will make you solve problems for the most people or big problems for few people will make you very valuable.

4. Become an Expert in Something

You have to be an expert to become valuable. According to a research, it takes about 10,000 hours of practices to become an expert of gain mastery of a field. That is like 7 to 10 years of learning and practice. An expert is the highest form of mastery of a field.

If you read a book in an area each month, you would have read 12 in a year, 24 in two years, 36 in 3 years, 48 in 3 years and 60 in 4 years. In 8 years you would have read 120 books. You will have a good understanding of the field you studied and have a lot of ideas. That will make you an expert.

Today most people just read a book and begin to behave like experts, no one can tell them anything. When you put them under pressure you will know they have no depth. Experts have depth in one field and shallow knowledge in many other fields.

Don't go out until you have become an expert. A pastor who decide to become an expert on faith, will have to read books and listen to audios on faith for years. Before you know he will begin to speak and operate in faith like no one else. He will become the known expert on faith. Many people are in a hurry to become to be known instead of becoming more valuable.

Work on yourself to become an expert. Experts impact people's lives. When you study a field, it becomes part of you because it has taken over your thoughts. Value, then, flows out of you like you are connected to the source of all water.

When you develop yourself in an area, you become better in it.

5. The Results You Produce

You can also increase your value by the results you produce. Valuable people always make things happen. They get the result they say they will get. If you are into giving excuses and blames, you will never become valuable.

Most people focus on just activities without any results. There is no way you can be busy and productive. You either are busy or productive. We tend to confuse activities with making progress and being busy with being productive. There are lots of people who are busy going nowhere and getting no results.

Peter Drucker said it this way, *"There are two types of people in the business community: those who produce results and those who give you reasons why they didn't."* When people tell me they are busy I know its just activities, putting in the motion with nothing to show for it. Being busy is just the excuse we give people for our lack of productivity.

There is no way you can increase your value when you are all talk and no action. If you will do your work with excellence, you will become very valuable to people. You have to aim at producing results that matters to people.

Results make you valuable. If you give in to producing results, you will always be increasing your value.

6. Be Different, Unique to Standout & Dominate

There are many people out there trying to show they are valuable, they have completely saturated the marketplace. You have to rise above their noise by standing out.

If you are like everyone, then you will be no different from anyone and you, your voice and value will be lost in the noise. You have to think different if you want to be different from others. If you are thinking like everyone is, you will do the same thing they are doing.

You can differentiate by having a unique combination of skills and the way you solve problems for people. This means that you should not just be an expert in one field. You can combine different fields. You can learn something from another industry and then bring it into your industry.

If there are people who can do the same thing that you can do, your value will be almost the same as all of them. That means you will never be the first choice. You have competitors and cannot dominate.

You are to standout and dominate and not just to be like everyone. You have to have a head taller than everyone so that you can be noticed above them. Your value should be so visible that everyone can see it.

When people are zigging, you should be zagging if you want to stand out. Do the opposite of what others are doing or even do more of it. Find out what the average performance is and then do much more than everyone in that field. You will become the dominating force in that field or industry. Do these and you will become valuable. Until you are valuable you will not be a Value Giver.

If you invest in yourself, you will never be the same. If you do it continually over time, you will become a better version of yourself. It is impossible to become better and not to become more valuable.

When you become a person of value, you will begin to help other people become better and you will become valuable. When you become better, everything around you get better.

You are like a tree: when you expose yourself to the right atmosphere and resources, you will grow and become better. And you will produce the kind of results that will add value to people.

CHAPTER TWO

GROWING YOUR CAPACITY

"Everything comes to us that belongs to us if we create the capacity to receive it." Rabindranath Tagore.

◆ ◆ ◆

The whole Value Giver concept is based on the fact that through us the whole families of the earth will be enriched and also that it is more enriching to give than to receive. We are not here on earth to just take care of our needs, but rather to help many people with their needs.

The philosophy of the Value Giver is that "No one can get rich unless he enriches others." If you think this is all about you becoming rich and accumulating everything while others serve you, then you have gotten the wrong book. The Value Giver philosophy is about being of service to people.

Value Givers give value or enrich people. You will only have your needs met when you help enough other people with their needs. You, therefore, need to always hide your needs and always be ready to help other people. You can never receive anything until you send something out.

There was a time when I used to blame the government and almost everyone for my lack. As I listened to Jim Rohn, I came to realize that nothing will come to me except I send something out. Earl Nightingale said, *"We've got to put the fuel in before we can expect heat."* Likewise, we've got to be of service first before we can expect money. Don't concern yourself with the money. Be of service. Build. Work. Dream. Create. Do this and you'll find that there is no limit to the prosperity and abundance that will come to you."

I was in lack because I was not serving anyone. My capacity to give was small or almost inexistent. Our capacity to give is the same capacity to receive. When you increase your capacity to give, so also your capacity to receive will increase.

There is no way you are going to enrich people without enriching yourself. There is no way you will shine light on people's path without you enjoying the same light. Value Givers make the place where they are better.

When you become a person of value, next thing is to start creating value for people. The good thing is that you can create value anywhere you are. You don't have to be the leader to create value. You can create value from any position. The only challenge is that most of us are limited by our capacity.

I had similar challenge years back. I really wanted to help my boss, but I just felt like something was holding me back and I could not just create more value than I was presently creating. I knew I could do more, but just didn't know how to go about doing it.

It was frustrating. I knew I could create more value but I just wasn't able to. My potential wasn't the challenge. Our potential is the same as that of God; unlimited. But our capacity is where the challenge is. It is limited.

You can do nothing to increase your potential but you can increase your capacity. The capacity places a limit on your potential.

You have the potential to earn all you want to earn but your capacity will hinder you you from doing that. You have to increase or expand your capacity to be able to unleash your potential. So to be a Value Giver, you have to constantly keep working on increasing your capacity

Your potential is channeled through the capacity you provide. If you increase your capacity, more of your potential will be unleashed. Your capacity can grow through use or shrink when not used. You are responsible to grow your capacity. No one will do it for you. It has to grow through intentionality.

Value Givers' creative activities is always to the benefit of many. The greater the number of value givers in a company or nation, the greater the benefit that flows to everyone. They create wealth for the common good. Their presence influences the standard of living positively. Nations like Nigeria that have few of them are often more impoverished and not making progress.

The best way for a company or nation to create an opportunity to become richer and developed is to deliberately nurture more Value Givers. That is can only happen when the mindset of people are transformed from takers to givers.

Transformed to Be a Value Giver

Let me share a secret Bishop Oyedepo taught me. He said, *"if I want to have a jet, I need to get to a place where I can create value that is equivalent to a jet."* It may sound simple but it's not all that simple. Thats because if you want to create that kind of value your focus should not be on the jet but to increase your capacity to give value.

Naturally, we are not people who want to give value to others. We prefer to receive than even give. Sometimes we give back to only people who give to us. Like children, we want to take and accumulate rather than give.

Everyone around you wants to take. At times you wonder if there are people who even think of just making it a lifestyle to give value to people each day. But there are. You too can become one.

Becoming a Value Giver starts from your mind. You should not conform to the way society expects you to behave but rather be transformed by changing your mind so you can understand that you can only receive the best things in life when you help people first.

To become a Value Giver, you will have to change how you think and what you do daily. To better understand this, order for my book, The Millionaire Maker. If you want to be a Value Giver, you will have to first change the way you think. Changing your thinking transforms you. However if you only change your thinking without changing the way you do things and the things you do, you will never be a Value Giver. You will still do things that makes you a taker.

The greatest challenge you will face is that of changing your mind. If you cannot change your mind, you will not be able to change anything you do. Surprisingly, when you change your mind and the way you think, then, the things you see changes.

Changing your mind will also result in the changing of your capacity. If you want to grow your capacity, you should start from changing your mind. Your capacity is equal to what you think. Whatever you think about, you become and you will also produce.

That counsel from Bishop Oyedepo made me think deeply and changed the way I think. I am still working on increasing my capacity so I can be able to create and give the kind of value that will bring me the equivalent of what I give. I have to upgrade my mind to increase my capacity.

When you expand your capacity to create and give value, you will need room enough for the things you are going to get back. If you are a good giver, you should also make ready your capacity to receive.

And to create any kind of value, you will have to first grow your capacity. Each day I work on my growing my capacity. I work harder on growing my capacity because it will determine what I get back. Giving starts the receiving process. Working to grow my capacity is my most important task.

What Keeps People's Capacity Low

There are 4 things that keep people's capacity low;

1. Your Belief

We end up unable to do because most of us believe that we cannot. When you believe that all you need to become rich is to know someone or get a good job, you will never invest in growing your capacity. Your belief, is what you will experience.

If you believe you cannot do something, your capacity will never grow. It becomes your self fulfilling prophesy. I have learned that when you believe you cannot do one thing, you will also believe that you cannot do other things. If you believe you can do something that is tough, then you will do anything that is tough. If you don't believe you can do something, you will never invest your effort, time and resources to grow your capacity.

Your daily activities determines what you believe. If you believe that your capacity is important to you creating and receiving value, you will do something daily to expand your capacity. If you don't believe, you will do nothing.

2. Environment

The environment you are living in matters a great deal. Whatever the people in that environment are doing, you will most likely do same. Your environment can limit your capacity

You need to be in a place where people are encouraging and are growing their capacity too. That way growing your capacity will be very easy for you.

You have no power over the environment you were born in but you sure have a choice to stay in that environment when you are old enough. If you stay with people who have a small capacity, chances are you also have a small capacity.

The people you associate influence your capacity. If you are doing everything to grow your capacity, but stay in a limiting environment, you will be mocked and laughed at because you are making the effort to get out.

Seek an environment where people are constantly expanding their capacity and will challenge you to do likewise. If you are not being challenged to expand your capacity, then you are in your comfort zone. Nothing hinders the expansion of your capacity like staying in your comfort zone. You are happy with mediocrity.

3. Small Thinking

If you are the type who think small then your capacity will be small. To grow your capacity you will have to think big. If you have to think at all, why don't you just think big?

You need to expand your thoughts so that you can unleash more of your potential. Your capacity is related to your thinking. If you want to expand your capacity, you will have to expand your thinking.

A couple of years ago I had a dream but I saw that dream as impossible. My thoughts was small. The dream was from my potential, but seeing it as impossible was from my thoughts. Whatever my mind cannot think of looks impossible. No one can do anything when the things looks impossible to you.

I thought prayer will make the difference but it was just an excuse for not investing in the expansion of my capacity. Fervent prayer cannot make what I see as impossible possible. Prayers cannot do for you what your mind cannot think about.

If you want to increase your capacity to create and give value, then you will have to expand your mind. As your mental capacity increases, you will have more ideas on how to create value.

4. Fear

Fear of the unknown and what people will say are part of the reason why most people hardly grow their capacity. Your capacity grows when you constantly face your fears and do the things that you think you cannot do.

Your capacity will keep growing when you keep doing what you have not done before. The more courageous you are, the bigger your capacity. Whatever you fear to do will shrink your capacity. That's why in my caching program, I ask people to do something they are afraid of or they think they can never do.

When you face your fears, the fear ends and your capacity expands in that area. Our fears most times are based on some rules that someone taught us when we were young. Some of the religious rules we fearfully follow have resulted in people have small capacities.

People with small capacities become takers instead of Value Givers. They don't believe they can create value and have nothing to give, so they keep taking. If someone is afraid of not having, there is no way that person will work to create more in order to give more. The person will believe that taking is the best thing to do.

There was a time when I was afraid of not having money, so when I have a few cash with me, I hoard it. Then I faced that fear. Anytime I have money that is not enough, rather than give in to my fears, I face the fear and use it to buy books. I prefer to have books to read than food to eat.

I faced the fear and my capacity to create more value and make more money has increased. Whatever you fear and think you cannot do shrinks your capacity.

Stretch To Grow Your Capacity

To grow your capacity, you have to stretch yourself by learning new things, doing the things you haven't done before and going to the end of yourself.

Normal doesn't stretch anyone. You have to go beyond your comfort zone to be stretched. When you seek towards an easy company, where you are not challenged and not pushed out of the comfort zone, you won't grow. And if you don't grow, you will definitely become a liability to the company instead of an asset.

You need to accept the counsel of Jim Rohn when he said, *"Don't see an easy crowd; you won't grow. Go where the expectations and demands to perform are high."* You can never be at your best except you are in an environment where you are constantly challenged to beat your last performance.

If there is no tension in your life, then you really will never grow. You have to stretch to grow. A life where you have arrived will never experience growth. I mean if there is nothing better to live for, why should you even grow? Just like a rubber band becomes useful only when stretched, so also you will be relevant when you are stretching. Stretching expands you.

You Will Never Realize Your Potential to Create Value Until You Stretch Yourself

When you stretch yourself, you will grow your capacity and since your potential is dependent on your capacity, you will realize it. Your capacity is like rubber band and only useful when it is stretched. It is a waste of your capacity to leave it the way it is.

God gave you the gift of his potential, your gift back to him is to put that potential to work. If you are not stretching your capacity, you will waste the potential.

To my amazement, I find out that the more I stretch myself the more I am able to do. Anytime I stop stretching, the things I can do remain the way it is. There is no limit to what I can do except the limitation set by my capacity. To do more I will have to stretch my capacity everyday.

You Will not Fully Know the Extent of Value you can Create Until you are Stretched.

That is the truth. You will never know what you can do and how far you can go except you stretch yourself and do what you have not done. If you think you have created the greatest value you can ever create then you have given in to self deception.

The greatest value you can ever create doesn't exist. Whatever you have done, you still can do more than that. There is no limit to what you can do. Whatever you have done is the starting point of what you can still do.

You Won't Effectively Create Value Unless You Stretch.

You have to go the extra mile if you want to effectively create value. Apple did not just create a phone, they stretched themselves and go beyond what is the normal and then created one of the greatest value ever created called the iPhone.

You have to first know the effect that you want to create and then stretch yourself to make sure that you produce the exact result that you want to create. You have to stretch to exceed people's expectation.

If you want to have the normal effect or result, then you will have to do the normal things that everyone does. But if you desire to do things differently and get better results, you will have to stretch yourself. Anyone who is getting the kind of results everyone is getting is not stretching. Stretching gives your value an edge over others.

When you stretch, you will produce excellent results. That way you are set apart from many people in the market. Go the extra mile in creating value and you will be set apart from many.

Your Potential to Create Massive Value gets Paralyzed when you are Afraid to Stretch.

Abraham Maslow, the American psychologist, said, "If *you plan on being anything less than you are capable of being, you will probably be unhappy all the days of your life.*" Fear has a way of keeping you at the level you have always been with a shrunk capacity. The more you stretch, the more the value you can create.

You can never rise beyond your fears when you are afraid to stretch. Fear imprisons your potential to create value. You have to constantly face your fears by challenging the status quo and breaking rules. The courageous create more value than the timid. Don't ever entertain fear when you are going to create value. Face your fears and do the things you fear most and you will be free to do more than you want to do. To overcome fear, love the people you are creating value for. Perfect love cast out fear.

You will only Create Better Value When You Stretch Beyond Where You are.

When you get better whatever you create will get better. So also when you improve as a person, the value you create will improve. It takes you stretching to become better and improve on the last value that you created. If you want to create better value, you must stretch.

You have to become restless and never be satisfied with what you have been creating. If you stop stretching and improving your value, you will one day find out that no one really need the value you are creating.

You don't have to wait till someone create a better value than yours. Make sure that you are constantly growing, and improving and the value you are creating will improve. Don't ever settle. Make yourself uncomfortable always.

To stretch to create better value, you have to do what you have never done before, do more than you have done, learn things you have never learned before. It takes courage to improve upon what you have done before.

Where You Stop Stretching is Where Your Relevance Stops.
The death of your relevance happens when you stop stretching. But as long as you are stretching and going beyond what you have done, you will remain relevant.

If you depend on what you created yesterday to be relevant, you will be shocked at how fast you will loose relevance. You have to stay in touch with people's needs and keep creating value to meet those needs. People's needs are always changing, so you have to keep stretching to create the value that will meet the needs.

When what you create stops meeting the needs of people, it is outdated. No value last forever. You have to stretch to anticipate the needs of the future and create the value that meet those needs.

You need to do the following in order to stretch:
- Never Accept Average
- Refuse to be Comfortable
- Take on Something Bigger Than Yourself

Capacities To Develop
To be a value giver there are certain capacities that you will need to grow.

Without these capacities, you will never be able to create much value or even deliver value. You can only deliver the value you created and no more.

1. Mental Capacity
This is your ability to think. The creation of value starts from what you think. The difference between people who give value and those who don't is really how they think.

Rich people are value creators and givers, while poor people are value seekers. Poor people are so focused on themselves and their needs that they are unable to focus on the needs of others.

Your thoughts is either creating or not creating value. You grow your mental capacity by reading books written by people who think bigger than you. When you read something new, you are growing your mind in that area.

If you want to create business value, you will have to read the books of people who are successful in business, so that your mental capacity can be built up to equal theirs. When you think about what they have written, your mind will get sharpened and your thoughts ungraded.

When you read books and listen to audios, you are building your mental capacity. Read a book and listen to an audio continuously until it has possessed your mind. That way your mental capacity will expand.

2. Leadership Capacity

This is the ability to work with and influence people to do what they thought they cannot do. Value creation involve people. If you don't know how to relate with people and inspire them to unleash their potential, your capacity to create and give value will be limited.

If you want to create massive value you will have to learn to work with other people. Alone there is a limit to what you can do but working with others you will create much more value.

You expand your leadership capacity by learning to connect with people and also communicate to them. Leadership is influence. You have to learn to influence people in order to create more value.

That's what leaders do. They connect with people, communicate a vision, influence people to buy into the vision and then inspire them to grow their capacity and together create massive value. Through the connection they are able to stir the heart of people and inspire them to do great things.

If you want to be a better leader then you have to learn to communicate to encourage and inspire people. The bigger your leadership capacity, the more the value you are going to create and contribute to people.

People who develop their leadership capacity help others do the same. When you start helping other people to develop their capacities, you are going to multiply the massiveness of the value you create.

The major work of leaders is to develop other leaders. That way they multiply the results that they produce. The more you grow your leadership capacity and longer you do it, the greater your capacity will be and the more people you will help become better leaders and the greater will be the value you are going to create.

3. Solution Capacity

This is the ability to solve problems for people. To create value you have to learn to solve problems and meet people's needs. The more people you can solve problems for the more value you can create. You need to develop your capacity for solutions and not problems.

Instead of developing capacity for solutions, most people are developing their capacity to avoid or run away from problems. All they discuss and think about is the problem they are experiencing and never the solutions they are going to come up with.

You will never wish away problems. As long as there are people there will always be problems. You either build your capacity to solve a huge problem for few people or solve a problem for many people. Developing solutions is what creating value is all about.

Remember value is in the eyes of the receiver. People determine what value really is to them. If they don't have the problem, so solution will mean nothing to them.

To grow your solution capacity you have to keep practicing solving problems and asking questions. I find out that each time I am able to question the problem and understand it better, the solution comes easy.

You solve problems where you ask the right questions. The kind of questions you ask will help you to define and reframe the problem. Framing it in the right context will help with coming up with the solutions.

Curiosity fuels your imagination. If you can ask questions, you will focus your imagination to come up with solutions for any problem. Imagination is the ability to invent, see and come up with solutions to problems.

The more you practice solving problems the better you become at it. To expand your capacity for solution to problems you have to learn to ask the right questions.

4. Production Capacity

This is the ability to turn nothing into something. It's the ability to start with nothing and create what people want. It is the place where you combine different factors and come up with value that people want.

You make things happen here. While other complain, people who develop their productive capacity are coming up with things that works and make life better for others.

People who have developed their productive capacities are re-sourceful. Your ability to produce results for people will determine the value you create. Jim Rohn said, "Human beings have the remarkable ability to turn nothing into something. They can turn weeds into gardens and pennies into fortunes." You can do the same if you will develop your production capacity.

You expand your production capacity by imagining all possibilities, believing that anything you can imagine is possible and then working it out. Production starts from imagination and ends with work. Imagination is the capacity to see what doesn't exist in reality yet.

If you are not ready to imagine impossible things and then take action to make it a reality, you will never expand your production capacity.

5. Empathy Capacity

Most of us only know how to sympathize with people and not how to empathize. People who sympathize with others cannot create value, but people who empathize do. Sympathy and empathy are variant of compassion but there is a difference between them.

When you sympathize with people, you kind of judge them but when you empathize, you don't. Empathy tries to understand the person, while sympathy behaves like it understands.

While sympathy is feeling for someone because of their challenge and what they go through, empathy is the ability to feel what the other person is feeling. When you empathize with someone, you put yourself in their shoes so that you can feel where the shoe pinches them provided you have the same shoe size.

Empathy is the ability to see things from the perspective of others and to feel what they feel. You have to know where the shoe pinches people, their pain points and real problems in order to create value for them. If you don't understand what people are going through, you will never know what they need.

People don't really know what they need so it's a waste of time to even try asking them. You have to get into their environment and observe them to really understand. Steve Jobs puts it this way, "Some people say, *'Give the customers what they want.'* But that's not my approach. Our job is to figure out what they're going to want before they do. I think Henry Ford once said, *"If I'd asked customers what they wanted, they would have told me, 'A faster horse!'"* People don't know what they want until you show it to them. That's why I never rely on market research. Our task is to read things that are not yet on the page."

Empathy helps you to know what people want even though they don't really know what it is.

To grow your capacity for empathy, you will need to care for people more and love them more.

6. Emotional Capacity

This is the ability to master your emotions and focus your emotions to believe in something strongly. It's called mental toughness.

Mental toughness is the ability to resist, manage and overcome negatives feelings that prevents you from creating value to serve people. Dr Peter Clough said, *"Mental toughness describes the capacity of an individual to deal effectively with stressors, pressures and challenges and perform to the best of their ability, irrespective of the circumstances in which they find themselves."*

It determines your capacity to handle doubt, discouragement and pressures as you work on developing value for people. You can never create value without faith. The person who is able to control her emotions will operate more by faith than the person who is controlled by his emotions.

Faith is very important when it comes to creating value. You need faith to create values that are incredible and impossible. When you believe all things become possible to you. People who expand their emotional capacity are confident people. You have to believe in yourself and be confident in your ability to create value.

You need to be mentally tough when trying to produce value for people. It will help you persevere and endure anything that will come your way. Anything that can happen to challenge you from creating value will happen. It can take longer than you plan and people may disappoint you along the way. You need to build your emotional capacity so that you can stay the course without deviating from your goal.

You can build your emotional capacity by constantly putting yourself under pressure. The more you can handle pressure, worries and doubt, the greater your performance and production will be.

One way I have found out that what really work is to tell everyone one what you plan to do. That way you put yourself under pressure to make it happen. It's hard to tell people about the value you want to create when you don't even have what it takes to create it. Doing so will help you manage your emotions.

So keep saying it and never relent. When you build your emotional capacity you will be able to stand anything to that looks impossible will become possible.

Building your emotional capacity makes creating value easy and fun.

So begin work on building and growing your capacities and you will see that it becomes easy for you to create value. If you work on yourself to develop your capacity to create and contribute value for people, you will unleash your potential and will add great value to people.

You can create more value. You can touch the lives of people and make things better for them. All you have to do is focus on growing your capacity and you will make a difference in people's lives.

CHAPTER THREE

DETERMINE YOUR INCOME

"You don't get paid for the hour. You get paid for the value you bring to the hour…We get paid for bringing value to the marketplace. It takes time,…but we get paid for the value, not the time." Jim Rohn.

◆ ◆ ◆

An eight-year-old boy went to his grandfather and proudly announced, "I am going to be very successful when I grow up. Can you give me any tips on how to get there?"

The grandfather nodded, and without saying a word, took the boy by the hand and walked him to a nearby plant nursery.

There, the two of them chose and purchased two small saplings. They returned home and planted one of them in the back yard. The other sapling was placed in a pot and kept indoors.

"Which one do you think will be the most successful in the future?" asked the grandfather.

The boy thought for a moment and said, "The indoor tree. It's protected and safe while the outdoor one has to cope with the elements."

The grandfather shrugged his shoulders and said, "We'll see."

The grandfather carefully tended to both plants and in a few years, the boy, now a teenager came to visit again.

"You never really answered my question from when I was a young boy. How can I become successful when I grow up?" he asked.

The old man showed the teenager the indoor tree and then took him outside to have a look at the towering tree outside.

"Which one is greater?" the grandfather asked.

"The outside one. But that doesn't make sense, it has to cope with many more challenges than the inside one."

The grandfather smiled, "Yes, but the risk of dealing with challenges is worth it as it has the freedom to spread its roots wider and its leaves towards the heavens. Boy, remember this and you be successful in whatever you do; If you choose the safe option all of your life you will never grow and be all that you can be, but if you are willing to face the world head-on with all of its dangers and challenges, the sky's the limit."

The young man looked up at the tall tree, took a deep breath and nodded his head, knowing that his wise grandfather was right.

When we face challenges, we grow. And when we grow we are able to determine the value we create and consequently the compensation. If you want it easy, you will never grow and will never be able to determine your income. This is the one thing that most people don't really believe but Value Givers know.

We understand that our income is based on the value that we bring to the marketplace. The truth is that you can determine your income since you can control the value you create.

Value Givers are in charge of their income. Because they believe that they can have the income they want, they are not in a hurry and not greedy.

When you see anyone who is in a hurry to make it, then you should know that the person isn't a value giver.

Myth About Compensation

Your salary is not determined by you, it is simply the value that your employer places on the position you are occupying not on the value you bring. The salary is the starting point though. You can use it to leverage your skills and produce value that will help you determine your income. There are many beliefs, misconception and myths people have about determining their compensation. Here are seven.

- **Experience Myth.** Many people believe that their compensation will rise simply because they have more years on the job. Employers, most especially in the public sector, promote their employees as a result of the years in service. Every promotion comes with an increase in salary. This is across board and not unique to anyone. Since you are not in control of the promotion, you definitely are not in charge of the compensation.

- **Education Myth.** Of course, the higher your educational level the more you are compensated. This I believe is more important in research centers and academics. Again, no matter the qualification, you cannot determine your income.

- **Location Myth.** There are cities you get to that pay more than others. Take for instance, New York or Silicon Valley, pay more than when you are in Abuja, Lagos or Accra. Inasmuch as the compensation in cities differ, someone determines how much you are paid not you.

- **Business Myth.** Most people who believe this end up with another job instead of a business. They may make some money but are not in control of what they make. Your salary can make you rich if you know how to leverage it. That other people have become rich through business doesn't automatically mean everyone can.

- **Luck Myth.** People don't determine their income by luck. They do so by design. I used to think that people who earn what they want are just lucky, but now I know that they got lucky because of their preparation and the value they keep creating. No one consistently earns what they want by accident; they do know by knowing and doing the things that puts them in charge of their income. Anyone can earn what they want if they can just be highly intentional about what they do.

- **Appearance Myth.** The way one looks doesn't in any way signify whether the person is rich or not. The way you dress is simply personal choice. I have met poor people who dress like they are rich and rich people who dress as if they have no money. If you are a poor who believe that you are addressed by how you dress, you will spend your money to look rich, thereby making someone richer.

- **Demand Myth.** Most employees believe that the best way to determine their income is to make demand for an increase in salary. No matter how much you demand that your income be increased, you will never be in control of what you earn; your employer will be. To determine your income, you have to do so by supplying value and not demanding for more. When you demand for more, you are just a taker.

Factors That Influence Your Compensation

There are Four Factors That Determine Your Income;

- Hours You Can Work

This limits your income because you have limited hours in a day. You cannot create more hours or days. The highest you can do to earn more is to work overtime and then ask for the time to be monetized. Anyone working for time deprives himself great opportunities. The person they are working for still controls what they earn.

So if you are paid by the time, you need to increase the time you work to increase your income. When you work for time, you income will be limited. This income is based on the desire for job security and guaranteed income. There is no risk involve in working for time.

Value Givers are not paid for the hours they work that is why they are always in control of whatever they earn. When you work for time you will never be able to determine your income. They leverage time, though, to create something that will determine their compensation.

- The Place You Work

The place you work also can determine what you earn. You are not in charge of what you earn. Each industry have a pay structure for its workers. So to some extent, the company you work for will determine what you earn.

If you want to earn more you will have to change company. That is what this means. People are envious of people who work in certain organization where the pay is great.

When people are looking for a job, they talk about how much the company pays. Here your income depends on the company you work for. Value Givers compensation doesn't depend on the place they are working; rather on what they do. They get compensated for the value they bring to the place where they work.

- The Position You Occupy

In any company, incomes are determined by the position you have. The employer attaches a certain amount as salary to each position in his business. Entry level have a certain salary and benefits, while management has its own. If you want to earn more you have to be patient to rise to the top of the food chain.

People who are on the lower rung of the ladder in an organization are always advised to wait their turn to enjoy the perks of the senior or management positions.

Strangely many people endure everything just because they want to reach the top and enjoy the benefits of being at the top. The only challenge is that the management positions are limited and not everyone can get there.

Value Givers don't get compensated because of the position they occupy but what they do as a result of the position they occupy. That is, the value they bring to that position.

- The Value You Create

When people say that you have to start a business to control what you earn, I know that they know next to nothing about money. You can start a business and others will be richer than you and not even determine your income.

To determine your income, you have to create the exact value that will produce how much you want to earn. People who create value enjoy expanded capabilities, capacities and unlimited opportunities.

You can determine your compensation if you can create its equivalent value. Value Givers get compensated for the value they create and contribute and not for time, company the work for or position they occupy. They focus on creating greater value and contributing massive value to their workplace and marketplace.

If you are not being compensated for the value you create and give, then your income is at the mercy of someone. What you are earning today should be the compensation for what you have contributed in the past. Value Givers don't work for time but they leverage and maximize time, the company they work for and the position they occupy to create results that is needed.

To increase your compensation, you must therefore increase the value of your contribution. Value Givers are paid based on their contribution to the workplace. They work to create value because they desire greater opportunity, income and freedom.

What to do to Control Your Income

The choice you make will determine what you get compensated with. The truth is that what you earn depend solely on you. You have more control than government and the economy of your nation. Your philosophy or what you believe about affects your income more than anything or anyone you can think of.

That's because what you believe determines the choices you make and the things you do. Here are what you can do to control your income;

1. Do More Than You Receive in Payment

You need to create more value so you can contribute more. You are not paid for the value you create but for the one that you contribute that makes a difference.

Most people either supply less or exactly what they are to be paid. You need to supply much more than that. Whatever you supply is based on what you believe you can supply.

If you want to earn more, then you will need to supply more value. Of course, you must create the value before you can supply it.

2. Provide the Cause, Enjoy the Effect

For every income you earn there is something you have to do. People don't become rich miraculously because getting rich is dependent on the law of sowing and reaping or cause and effect.

Whatever you get is based on something you first gave out. Giving starts the receiving process. Whatever you send out will determine what comes back to you.

God can never be deceived so don't deceive yourself to think that you will reap without first sowing something. When you sow maize seed, you will definitely reap maize crops for harvest. You will never get back what you have not first given.

Your income is an effect and you are in charge of the cause. It doesn't matter where you are; you can earn what you desire if you will just do what needs to be done. Find the cause and do it and you will certainly reap.

3. Serve More People and Serve Them Well

The more people you create value for and supply value to, the more you are able to earn. If you want to earn a billion dollars, you can. All you have to do is create and supply value to millions of people or even a billion. Just get to solve the problem that affects millions of people.

Whatever you want to earn, just make sure there are people who need what you are supplying and then monetize and supply it to them. Peter Diamandis, the co-founder of Singularity University and author of Abundance, says, *"The world's biggest problems are the world's biggest business opportunities… You want to be a billionaire? Find a billion-person problem that you can make a dent in."* You can control what you earn if you can serve more people and serve them exceptionally well.

4. Placing Other People's Interest First

If you want to control your income then you will need to place the interest of other people above yours. You will only have your needs met when you meet the needs of others. If you are only interested in what you can get, you will only have crumbs.

To be able to earn what you want you will need to help as many people with what they want. If you are focused on your need, there is so much you can earn meeting your need. That's how people become greedy.

Value Givers spend their whole time fixated about the needs of others. They work to come up with a better solution for the needs of people. That way they are in control of their income. Understanding this will help you a great deal.

5. The value you place on yourself

If you place value on yourself you will determine the value people will be willing to pay for what you supply. Just as thunder always come after lightening, so money comes after value is added. Money, therefore, is the thunder of values lightening.

You cannot create value for people except you first value yourself. When you value yourself you will invest in your capacity and capability to be able to solve problems for people. If you value yourself, you will value people.

Your value in the eyes of people is based on how much you value yourself. To value yourself, you have to be confident about yourself. You will not be able to do anything for people except you first believe in yourself.

If you look down on yourself, people will look down on you. If you price yourself cheaply people will do the same to you. No one can devalue you without your consent. When you value yourself, you will be priced the value you created rightly.

Signs That You Know Your Value

1. You Are Confident:

You are comfortable with who you are and what you can do. You accept yourself and are ready to improve yourself. Confidence is a proof that you see value in yourself and believe that you have something to offer people, the marketplace and the world that will make things better. Confident people are always investing in themselves to cultivate their value so as to be valuable anywhere they go.

People who give excuses, blame others and criticize people don't believe in themselves. They believe others are better than them. Others may only look better if you stop looking at yourself and seeing the value that you have. Everyone is unique but we just have to find out what makes us unique and that unique value that we can bring to people. When you find that, your confidence will soar.

2. You Recognize the Difference You Make in People's Lives

If you are ashamed about knowing and talking about your impact in people's lives, you don't believe you have value. It is not humility, but pride, when you cannot acknowledge the particular impact that you can make in people's lives. That is where you have the greatest value.

But if you can acknowledge the effect of what you create on people, then you can do more of it and impact people. You shouldn't just acknowledge it, you should tell people about it. It is the benefit they derive from doing business or relating with you.

Most people think that only businesses should do that. You are your own product and in every relationship, you know the benefits you are going to bring to the table. Telling people about the benefit of associating with you or your employer the benefit of employing you is a sign that you know and believe you have value.

3. You don't Envy People but Rather Learn from Them

If you envy anyone for what they have, you simply do not believe you have value. You will never create unique value because you will think the other person is better than you. You need to know that the grass doesn't just get greener on the other side by itself; people work at it to make it so. If you envy others for the value they give, it means you haven't been working on yours. You can only work on your value when you believe you have value.

No one is better than you. The value you create must be unique and standout for it to earn you what you desire. Stop focusing on how other people are valuable and start working on yourself to become valuable. You don't have to be like them because you are not like them. You are you. You should be able to accept yourself the way you are. Until you do that, you will never be able to see value in yourself and then work on yourself to become valuable.

4. You Don't Try to Impress People but Serve Them

If you are trying to impress people, you don't believe you have value. Value Givers serve people with the value that they create. They don't try to impress anyone. I have always avoided any chance to impress people. There is no way I will be impressing people while expressing my value at the same time.

We are all here to serve people and not to impress them. Service to people is the rent we pay for being on earth. It's the way to greatness. No one has ever made life better for others by impressing them; but when we serve people, we seek to make life better for them.

Most Nigerians don't really understand what it means to serve. We want people to serve us. Politicians who are elected to serve people become the lords that people have to serve. No society will ever make progress when people don't believe they have value to serve people.

Services is not a sign of weakness but a sign of confidence that you know you have value. Only the secured and strong serve, that's because they believe in themselves and see value in themselves.

5. You Don't Undercharge for Your Service

When you undercharge for your value because you want to get money, you are not helping your value. I have had to walk out from deals because I felt my value is being undermined. Of course, no one can undermine my value without my full consent and contribution. That is why I walk out of it. When your value gets undermined, it remains like that in your eyes and in the eyes of others.

You have to believe in the value of what you are bring to the table that you don't compromise on it. My advice to anyone who come to me about making money is never to do anything for money. Once you accept to do things for money, you will undermine your value by undercharging for the service you render.

Walking away from deals that require you to undercharge your services, will build up your confidence more and will send a signal that you really know what you are worth. I deliver massive value so I don't negotiate on price. And I keep telling people that as the value I create grows, so also what's in charge for my value. You should never be ashamed of your value.

6. You Know Your Strength, How Good You Are

People who know their value focus on their strength and not their weaknesses. From your strength will your value rise and not your weakness, so spend time working on your strengths and not just your weaknesses.

Where you have strength may be the weakness of many people including your competitors. Build your value around your strength and you will always draw a circle around others. For long I have invested so much in developing my strength and become valuable in it, now people assume I am strong in many areas. That is because my strength is compensating for my weakness. I still have those weakness and know what they are.

Stay in the area of your strength. That is the place where you will be valuable.

7. You Don't Work for Money but For Impact

If you know your value, you will never work for money or time. You will focus on creating things that will transform people's lives. People who do not know their value work for time, while those who do leverage time to create value. If you don't know your value, you will be part of the 80% of the workforce that share 20% of the compensation.

It takes time to create value, but once it is created, it will be a time well spent. People who create value are focus on others and not just on themselves. They understand that when they create value that meets the needs of others, their own needs will be met. So they are always obsessed with creating things that makes life better for others.

Anyone who spends time working on how to make life better for people knows his or her value.

What To Do to Determine Your Income

I have studied rich and successful persons for 20 years and one thing I know for sure is that their income is determined by them and not by any genie. They are in control of what they earn. They know exactly what they need to do to earn what they need to earn. I termed them Value Givers. Anyone can determine their income if they want to. From them I gleaned how to determine my income.

1. Determine How Much You Earn

You don't earn anything by accident. People who depend on earning an amount by chance don't really know their value. If they do believe in themselves they will decide what they want to earn. If you work for someone based on the time spent there, you won't be able to determine your income. Your employer will.

The first thing Value Givers do to earn what they want is to determine the exact amount they want to earn. If you don't know what you want to earn, you will settle for any amount. They don't set the amount because they want it but for what it will make of them.

For instance, I told myself that I want to earn $40, 000 a month in personal income. The money is not the goal but who I will become. That is more beneficial and important to me. That means I will have to work on myself to be able to create value of that amount in a month.

So what is it you want to be earning? Look at yourself and decide. Set something that will challenge you to become more than you are so you can create more value.

2. Why Do You Want To Earn That Amount?

Next decide the reason you want to earn. For me, it is because I want to travel the world. So I believe with that amount I can travel every month. This also means that the amount should be passive income. I mean, I want to earn the money even when I am traveling the world.

When your why is big enough you will be able to endure anything to achieve the why. Most people give up easily when things get tough because their why is not compelling enough. My why is enough to make me do whatever it will take to really earn the amount I determine to earn.

You have to set a compelling reason why you want to earn that amount of money. If you don't have a compelling reason, you won't give it all that it takes because it will not be worth it.

3. Who is Earning That Amount or Living That Lifestyle

Then next thing I need to find out is who are the people or persons earning that amount. The reason for this is that they already have the kind of mindsets and habits that are producing the value that brings them that amount.

Once you know who they are, next is to begin to read their books and articles and listen to them. The goal and objective here is to get to know and install their mindset, belief system and habits. You will only be able to produce the kind of results they are producing if you know exactly what they are thinking, believe and do daily to produce the amount.

Whatever they say they did, do it too. As you listen to them over-and-over, your mindset and beliefs will begin to change to be like theirs. Learn from them and model their mindset, beliefs and habits.

The value you create is based on your mindset, beliefs and habits. The more you model and learn from someone, the more you pick their kind of psychology and create their kind of value. Success always leaves clues. You will begin to think at their level and create value too. That way you are growing to be like the person.

4. Begin to Create Value

First, start creating value that the other person creates. You can start by copying them and replicating what they are doing.. The goal here is to gain mastery over whatever you create.

That was my aim when I started by creating the same value of Bishop Oyedepo by writing about him. When people got impacted, I knew that my mindset and beliefs are now at a level closer to his. I was modeling his thoughts and mindset. When I got to that level, I then channeled my psychology to creating unique value.

As I continually create value with that modeled psychology, it's just a matter of time and I will start earning at the level he is earning. That's because the value I am creating is at the same level as his. The value you create determines the amount you earn.

If you can think, believe and act like someone you will definitely produce their kind of value and earn what they are earning. Location is immaterial. Your psychology is all that matters. So work on your psychology and create value from that level.

Immerse yourself totally in the books and teaching of people you want to create value like and when your psychology changes, the value you create will also change to reflect that change in psychology.

CHAPTER FOUR

MULTIPLY YOUR VALUE

◆ ◆ ◆

Jerry Ankeli just got a job in Abuja with a company. He was given three months probation to prove his worth and value to the company. So after studying the company, he came up with a plan to demonstrate how valuable he is.

He first created a plan for all digital assets of the company, then a data bank for all contacts, and made sure all websites of the company, its subsidiaries, and business units were optimized. When I interviewed him, he said, "The result was great, because we now have a stronger digital presence, engagements across all digital channels, among others... When I started I had three months to prove what I can do and in which case, my contract would end but upon a satisfactory review, My services were confirmed."

That was what they need but didn't know they need. So by solving the problem for them, he demonstrated value and as a result got his employment confirmed before the 3-month probation period elapsed. He can multiply that value to become more valuable to his employer.

After value givers have created value, the next thing they do is to multiply that value

To multiply your value is to become highly value to few people or to spread out value to many people. Value is your ability to meet the needs of people. It is about sharing and distributing value to reach the people who really need it.

Value Givers are valuable to people that matters to them. If you are not increasing your value, you will get to a point where you are not relevant and valuable because you are now obsolete. That you are a valuable spouse doesn't mean you are going to be a valuable employee. You have to develop yourself in any area that you want to be valuable in.

You have to keep reinventing your value to stay relevant. People's needs are always changing. That you are valuable yesterday doesn't mean you will be valuable today. If you are valuable to one person, then you can start thinking of multiplying your value to more people.

If one person is going through a particular challenge, it means there are more people going through it. If you can help one person meet his or her challenge, then you can help more people with it. So spend your time developing solution for the problem one person is going through, then use that same solution to solve the problem of many.

This is the same principles at play when businesses produce their products. They first start with a model and once they are sure it solves a problem, they then multiply the value they have created to reach more people.

What To Do To Multiply Your Value

1. Focus on What People Want & Multiply Your Influence

The best way to influence people is to know what they want and then provide it for them. When you focus on what people want and then provide it for them, you are going to become more influential in their lives.

Quite a number of employees continually wonder how they can become influential in their workplace. There is no workplace that doesn't have a challenge. If you focus on the problems of your employer and provide the solution, you will multiply your influence with your employer.

I worked for a company some years back that had problems with revenue, client acquisition, and customer satisfaction. I focused on solving that problem. Within 7 months of executing my plan, things change for good. Then I approached my employer that I will be resigning. He dissuaded me from resigning and increased my salary without me asking. That's influence.

You have to find a way to know what they really need and want. It's your responsibility to always know what the needs are in the place you are in. You have to be on the look out for the problems where you work. Providing what they don't need will never make you an influencer.

2. Focus on What You Want and Multiply Your Mindset

If you focus on what you want you will invest in your mindset because your attitude will determine how far you go and your mindset what you produce or create. People don't start investing in their value until they want something for themselves.

Your value will multiply when you increase your mindset. To multiply your mindset means to expand its context and content. If you want to multiply your value, you have to first expand your mind and leverage its power to produce value.

If you don't know what you want, you will never invest in multiplying your mindset. You will allow your mindset to remain the way it is. There is no way anyone can multiply their value with the mindset they currently have if it's not helping them do that.

3. Focus on Strategy & You Will Multiply Your Progress

If you want to make progress have a strategy but if you want to multiply that progress you will have to focus on executing the strategy. The strategy will make you create the right value for people.

Most people who want to be rich and influential don't even have a strategy. They submit to luck and chance. How can anyone ever create value for people without a strategy? It's impossible. From experience, I learned that you can get out of any challenge when you have a strategy. It's not enough to have a strategy, you have to be committed to executing the strategy.

Value Givers have a vision of what they want to do in the life of people and then obsessively are committed to executing the strategy to make that happen.

4. Focus on Alone Time & Multiply Productivity

If you want to increase your productivity you will need to spend more time alone. Some do it as yoga, but I call it solitude; a time you spend alone. It allows you to reboot your brain and to connect to the most important thing in your life. Your brain gets a chance to rest and replenish Itself. I am able to focus on the most important thing after every solitude and my productivity always soars.

I have also found after time spent on solitude, I am able to focus more and most importantly to know intuitively what to do to get the results I want to have.

This is really working for me. The more time I stay alone, the more empathic I become and the more ideas I have on how to really help people have their needs met. That means bye spending time alone, I increase my ability to multiply my value to people.

5. Focus on Relationships & Multiply Opportunities

If you focus on building relationship with the right people, you will get a lot of opportunities to add value to people. Those you know can help you multiply your value to get to places you may never have imagined it will get to.

There are people who will never do anything to open door for another. It's all about them. I have discovered that the more people you know, the more opportunity you get to add value to more people.

You have to value people to build great relationships that will multiply your opportunities to be influential and add more value.. John Maxwell says, *"To build great relationships, you need to want more for people than you want from people. The people who want more for others and give more than they take are pluses. The ones who want and take more than they give are minuses."* Value Givers build great relationships and that is why they multiply their value through the many opportunities those relationships bring to them.

Don't take any relationship for granted. They may know someone who knows someone who can help you massively multiply your value. If you build friendship with generous people, opportunities will be multiplied for you. The people you meet in life and build relationships with will greatly determine the quality and quantity of opportunities you get.

6. Focus on Delegation & Multiply Income

If you focus on delegating what you are not good at or have strength in, you will increase your focus on what you can do better and by so doing will multiply your income. As easy as this sound, most people prefer to focus on doing what they have no strength in.

There are things you can do but they are just a distraction to you. You need to delegate what is not directly responsible for the value that you want to create so that you can focus on what directly affects the value you create.

Delegation makes you more efficient in creating value when you assign task to people who have skills that are better match for tasks that would have distracted you from producing value at the top of your craft. Robin Sharma always says, "*Addiction to distraction is the death of creative production.*" You have to stop doing work that doesn't matter and focus on the ones that really matter.

Most of us want to be known as people who can do almost everything and as such we get so distracted. We live in a highly distracted world where people find it hard to really focus on what is important. The cure is to delegate so you can focus on what matters. Focus expands your result.

7. Focus on Strength and Multiply Performance

Your performance is based on what you can do. So if you do more of what you are good at, you will increase what you are doing. When your performance multiplies as a result of focusing on your strength, your value will in turn multiply.

The challenge is that most people are average in everything so they are unable to really distinguish what they are good at and that which they are not. When you identify your strengths and focus on them, you will be more productive, perform better and be more engaged.

Once you know what you are good at, your strength, just make sure you become the best in the world in it. You have to own your craft and game by developing yourself to be the very best. When you become the best at what you do well, your performance will surge and your value will get multiplied. Be focused on your strength and gain mastery in it. It takes discipline to gain mastery but it is worth it.

Just try this and see how much value you will multiply. Get to know what you have strength in doing and just do that alone and keep improving, you will not only get better at it but your performance will also go through the roof.

8. Focus on Learning & Multiply Your Growth

You can multiply your value when you grow. You grow when you learn something new. When you grow, the value you create will also grow. I like as Jim Rohn puts it. He said, *"You can't achieve beyond your level of development. You don't achieve goals. You grow into them."* If you want to multiply your growth, then you need to increase your learning.

Growth is the focus of learning. The more you learn, the more you grow and the more you can do and produce. The only guarantee you have that your value will continually multiply is to keep learning new things and growing. When you stop learning, you stop growing.

To multiply your value, you will have to increase the rate at which you work on yourself. If you work harder on yourself than on any task, you will grow and produce more value. Multiplying your value depends on your focus to learn something new each day.

To surpass the value you created yesterday, you have to learn something new today. Social commentator and philosopher Eric Hoffer said, *"In a time of drastic change it is the learners who inherit the future. The learned usually find themselves equipped to live in a world that no longer exist."*

To learn is not just to read a book. It's more than that. You have to read, think, gain insight and apply it. Applying it complete the learning curve. What you cannot apply you haven't really learned.

The more you learn, the more you grow and the more your value increases.

9. Focus on Capability & Multiply Results

The more focused on your capability, the more ability you have between the results you produce. If you want to make more impact, then develop more skills and improve the skills that you have. The better you are at a skill, the better the results that you are going to produce. You capability is your ability to produce results that matters.

Great results comes with a unique combination of new skills. When you are able to do something so well, things will certainly get better around you. Whatever new value you want to create requires new, specific capabilities that you need to build. Your results create your impact. The truth is that lasting impact hinge on continually developing new capabilities.

The needs of people should determine which capabilities you need to build. It should be a high strategic priority of anyone who wants to be a Value Giver. People who have no skills can hardly produce the kind of results that people desire.

It is not just enough to learn new skills, you need to gain mastery in those capabilities if you want to multiply your value. Average competence will never get you the maximum results. Maurice Young said, *"To become a master at any skill, it takes the total effort of your heart, mind and soul working together in tandem."* You have to give it your all to master capabilities. And when you do, the results will be great.

Capabilities that will help you take small steps and do small things consistently will produce amazingly massive results over time. You should never look down on a capability. When you produce massive results, it's easy to multiply your value. So combine your capabilities with consistent action and see massive results coming over.

You need to work more on your skills sets to produce better results and multiply your value.

10. Focus on Courage & Multiply Wealth

When you are courageous, you will increase your capacity. You are going to create and give value in accordance to your capacity. You will never create value that is more than your capacity. Value equals wealth. So if you focus on increasing your capacity, it will affect what you do for people and what you get back in return.

The size, quality and quantity of the value you create is based on the size of your capacity. With a big capacity, you can create massive value for people and also get massive returns. To create great value takes courage which is, of course, dependent on a great capacity.

It is tough to create massive value for people. If you are not courageous to take a leap into the unknown, you will not be able to multiply your value. Robin Sharma says, "*Leadership requires great courage. It is tough to have to take the road less travelled on when everyone urges you to be like everyone else. It is tough to create your life on your own terms when others are telling you how your life should be created. But nothing will fill your heart with a greater sense of regret than lying on your deathbed knowing that you did not live your life and do you dreams.*" Courage will push you to create more value when others are holding back.

Wealth favors the courageous. Courage will make you do what others will not do. Wealth will always result when you do what others will never do. It takes courage to multiply wealth.

Focus therefore on increasing your capacity to multiply what you give and get in return.

How To Multiply Value

1. By Innovation

This is the combining of things that already exist to come up with something new in order to serve people better. Your ability to solve problems for people and doing it in a way that is new and unique will multiply your value to new heights.

For instance, there is nothing new about the iPhone, it's just a combination of things that already exists. Apple scaled the value of the phone by creating a phone that significantly meets the needs of people.

You can multiply your value by taking what you learn in an industry and bringing it to another industry. You copy or adopt to adapt. That's equally what innovation is.

Using your imagination is essential to innovation. The more you use your imaginations, the easier it is for you to come up with innovative ideas. Innovations makes it easy to multiply your value using less effort. To remain valuable you have to keep innovating because nothing will stay relevant except it gets better.

The needs of people are changing and when your value meets a need, it creates other needs for people. You have to make sure that the solution you create for people is continually meeting their needs and solving their problems. Your have to stay in tune with what people are going through to know exactly what problem they need solution to.

To multiply your value and stay relevant, you will have to let go of what met the needs of people yesterday. You have to continually innovate around people's needs to remain successful and cutting edge.

The challenge we normally have is when it comes to letting go of what worked yesterday for what will help people today. If you are satisfied with what you did yesterday, you will become irrelevant to people. Roger von Oech said, "It's easy to come up with new ideas; the hard part is letting go of the things you have loved and that worked for you two years ago, but will soon be out of date."

- **Study Trend**

Trend is a good place to look out for opportunities. Trends reveal the changes on the horizon that will help you create a value that will impact people more. You need to know the following about change:

Change is inevitable

Change is continual

Change create opportunities

You will only be relevant and multiply your value when you are taking advantage of the change and also are the one initiating the change rather than tagging along the change.

- Identify Opportunties

When changes happen opportunities abounds. But you have to be able to spot the opportunity that will help you create value that you can multiply. You have to be observant and listen well to see opportunities. When it is opportunity that everyone sees, chances are, it is crowded and saturated with value. You have to develop an eye for opportunities so that you will be able to see them long before anyone. That way you will be ahead of everyone.

- Meet Needs

Whatever you create if it doesn't meet the current needs of the people it is not innovation. You have to focus on the needs of people. Creativity can be about a wild ghost chase, but innovation is about the needs of people. The more people who needs you meet, the easier it is to multiply the value you create. The challenge, therefore, is to focus on the pains points of people and the problem they want solutions for.

This way you can multiply your value.

2. By Improvements

This means to make the value you have created better, faster, cheaper and/or within the reach of people. If you are not improving your value, someone else will be and they will soon make your value obsolete. If you want to achieve this you will need to make it a habit to introduce small, gradual improvement in your value.

The need of people are changing, so you need to continually improve yourself and the value you created so that you will keep meeting the needs of people. People are dynamic and so also are their needs. They are constantly evolving which means their needs are too.

Most people take for granted small daily improvements. They see it as insignificant. At least I did until I got to experience the compounded effect over time. Over time, small changes become huge. But when you wait to make all the improvements at once, it will overwhelm the people and they will certainly resist it.

If your value is blunt, it will not make much difference. You will need to sharpen it. When sharpened it will make more impact.

· **Get Feedback**

You should not blindly improve your value. You need to improve with inputs from the people you are serving. Deliberate improvement is when you get feedback from the people you are serving about the areas you should improve your value on. You can get feedbacks by observing them, getting completely immersed in their culture and environment and listening to them attentively.

· **Define What To Improve**

It is not everything that you should just improve. You have to define exactly what needs improvement at each point. When you just improve for the sake of improvements, you will end up rendering your value useless to the people. You may improve something they found useful and make it not useful. Improvement may mean removing something rather than just adding something. You have to know exactly what will meet the needs of the people you are serving so as your improvement will serve them better.

It is difficult to improve your value when you don't know:

What people found valuable

What part is a distraction from the value

What needs to change

· **Improve Your Mindset & Skills**

Every improvement will require an upgrade in your thoughts and skills. If you maintain the same mindset and skills, you will think your value is great as it is. As you improve your mindset, you will discover areas to change (what needs to be added and subtracted to make it more useful). As you improve your skills, you will be able to do exactly what needs to be done to make the improvement happen.

3. By Scaling

This means that you do more of what you are already doing that people find valuable to them. It is replicating what you already have so that you can reach more people.

For instance, an author writes a manuscript and then the manuscript is published into a book and mass produced. Also a singer can produce the master album of her songs and then mass produce it for more people. That is how to scale your value.

Microsoft scaled its value and made Bill Gates the richest man on earth. They developed a program and then copy it to a CD and then sold it all over the world. That way their value was able to be multiplied.

Scaling means to increase the size and volume of whatever you are doing. Whatever will help you increase the volume of your value, will call your value. When you scale your value, you will be able to make it rise above the noise and attract people's attention. That is you do what you have been doing in a much bigger scale and volume.

You have to replicate what has worked. Replication needs a system to work. To scale, you need to have a system. If you don't have a system, it will be hard to scale the value. To multiply your value, you have to depend on systems.

When you have a system in a place, you will always predictably and repeatedly create and multiply your value without much effort. Michael Gerber, author of The E-Myth, says that systems permit ordinary people to achieve extraordinary results, predictably. However, without a system, even extraordinary people find it difficult to predictably achieve even ordinary results."

Give Value For Free

To multiply your value by scaling, you have to learn to give out your value for free to people. If you want something to move round and get to a lot of people, give it out for free. Make sure it's something that really meets the needs of people.

I did that with some of my books and I am amazed at how people who I will never have reached call to tell me that they read my book and it helped them. Whatever kind of value you created for people, try and share them freely. Apple does that in its Apple stores. People are allowed to play with their devices and even check emails, browse the internet and take pictures.

Whatever you give will always return back to you in multiplied value. If what you gave meets the needs of people in a unique way be sure that you have just triggered work of mouth.

Give More Value

You have to create wow. You do that by going beyond the expectation of whoever you are serving with your value. The best
investment you can make in the value you created is to ensure
that you give more to people than you receive in payment. On the
extra mile, there is no traffic jam.

Value Givers are ready to give and do more for people they
are serving. When you exceed people's expectation, you delight
them. People who are delighted by what you do will definitely
tell others about you. It may not be that easy to do that, but when
you do it puts you ahead of competitors in the mind of people you
are serving.

It is good for business to do more for people. It is an investment in
your future.

Use Multiple Platforms

To scale your value, you will need platforms to reach more
people farther than you can. A platform is a place you stand on to
reach more people. And when you use multiple platforms, you get
to reach more people with your value.

The platform will amplify whatever value you have created. And
when it is amplified, more people will get to know about your
value. There are many platforms today you can use that are free
and easy to learn. Standing on those platforms, you can maximize
the value you have created.

If you can do these, you will be able to multiply your value

4. By Leverage

Leverage means multiplying your value with less effort. You get
to do more while applying little or no effort at all. The truth is,
there is a limit to the value you can multiply on your own. It will
require you to work smarter and not harder. The more leverage
you create and use, the more you are going to multiply the value
you created.

Leverage is the ability to create more value and reach more
people with less effort and resources. It enables you to build more
value and multiply it than you could ever achieve alone by util-

izing resources that extend beyond your own. It enables you to multiply value without being restricted by your personal limitations.

If you are not using leverage to multiply your value, you will be working harder doing less and getting less results. The more leverage you add, the more people you are going to reach. If you don't have a leverage, people will not get to hear about your value or even try it. And if you have no leverage, you will be someone's leverage to multiply their value.

Leverage Your Mind

The first and most important leverage you need is your mind; your ability to think and come up with ideas is the single lever that you need to start making things work and multiply your value. For your mind to be your lever to multiply your value, you have to continually invest in it to make it better.

You ability to think and come up with ideas will go a long way in helping you reach more people than just wishing that opportunities will appear. Opportunities are seen with their mind and not with the eyes. If you don't invest in your mind and program it to see opportunities to multiply your value, you will never see it. The mind filter of anything it has not been programmed with.

You have to learn to increase your knowledge base and also expand the capacity of your mind. You will only be able to add more value if you are able to invest in your mind by expanding it. If you want to add more leverage, expand the capacity of your mind.

Leverage People

Another word for leveraging people is leadership, it is the ability to influence people to do more than they ever imagined to do. To leverage people, you will have to become a better leader. When you leverage people, you are leverage their time, talents, expertise and experience. Just know that you cannot manage people, you can only lead them.

Leaders touch people's heart first so they can be able to leverage people's talents, expertise and experience. If you are not a better leader, you will not be able to get much from people. It's not enough to just get them to use their skills. You need people to pour their heart into helping you multiply value. That can only happen when you learn to value them and inspire them.

The work of a leader is to develop other leaders. So the more leaders you develop, the more you are going to multiply your value. When you leverage followers, you will only experience increment in your value and be limited by who you reach and influence with your value. But when you develop and leverage more leaders, you are going to reach much more people. Leaders will help you multiply your value.

Leverage Technology

Technology can simplify, automat and quicken many things you do and also boost the creation, scaling and multiplying of value. There are many tech platforms and channels you can leverage to reach the world with your value. You can use your phone, without moving an inch to market your value to everyone in the world. You can do that through platforms like Facebook, WhatsApp, Instagram, Snapchat, Twitter, YouTube and blogs.

Everything has really come down to the use of phone right now. The phone has more processing power than the super computer available some years ago. You can literally reach billions of people easily through your phone now. It is really amazing.

If you leverage technology to scale and multiply your value, you have a better chance of reaching more people. You can do almost anything online to reach your audience. Technology is there for your benefit; use it well.

5. By Partnership

Partnership is an arrangement where you and others agree to work together to multiply the value you created. You can only go so far alone, but with partnership, you can leverage the reach and influence of others. Mother Teresa said, "I can do things you cannot, you can do things I cannot; together we can do great things." Other people can help you multiply your value than you could do alone.

You will never unleash you potential maximally and reach much more people than you can imagine without collaborating with partners. I recently gave out an ebook for free and it literally went around the world without much effort from me. People just kept sharing it. They were my partners and collaborators in sharing the value that I created.

You don't start a partnership for what you can get out of it without giving. You have to find a common ground and place the needs of your partners as top priority. People will want to help you when they know they have a part in whatever you are doing. As a Value Giver, you have to also give value to whoever you partner with as they help you. There should be something for them.

You must make sure that you never violate the trust of your partners. They trust you that is why they are partnering with you. Say what you mean and mean what you say. Be an open book to them. Avoid having skeletons in the cupboard when partnering with people. When such skeleton is discovered, it could end the partnership and you will be the loser.

Connect to Influencers

In every industry there are influencers who you can leverage to reach more people. Here you will be renting their credibility and influence. You must make sure that what you are bringing to the table is exactly what it is. I have had the experience where what a partner said his product will do wasn't what it did. I had to stop the partnership and apologize to people I influenced.

Influencers are everywhere. Locate them and partner with them. They are bloggers, on social media and many other places.

Be Trustworthy

If you want to scale your value, you have to prove to people that they can trust and rely on you. You must not be in it just for what you can get but for what you can contribute and how you can help the other person achieve his or her goal also. If your focus is yourself, you will never build trust with anyone.

People you partner with can be a great leverage to multiply your value. You have to first leave your world to find a common ground with them and build trust. Trust is the oxygen that keep partnership fires burning. People will do more for you, and go to any length for you because they trust you.

CHAPTER FIVE

WALK IN PEOPLE'S SHOES

◆ ◆ ◆

A client once engaged my services to design a school system for him. He must have had a system expecting a building design but instead I went for the software of the school rather than the hardware. I requested that I visit the place where the school was to be built. My goal was to see the world from the perspective of people he is trying to help. Seeing the world from their point of view will really help in building a school that will work for them.

Visiting and observing them really placed me in a position that I felt I was designing the kind of school that I will also be attending. As I entered into their world, it became a major part of me. Now I understand what kind of school system they need to be part of. I was no longer designing it for them; I was doing it for me. I got to know what he needed because I empathized with them.

It's called empathy, Walking in People's Shoes. To create value for people, you will have to leave your own world and enter into the world of the people with a non-judgmental mind so that you can see the world as the people see it even if it is way different from the way you see your world.

Empathy is not about listening to what the people you want to create value for are saying. It's much deeper than that. It is observing them while they are talking for cues that will lead you to understand what they are saying without putting it into words.

People generally don't know what they want until it is presented to them.

You need to empathize with people if you want to add value to them much more than they expected. If you don't know how they feel, you will never know what they value. It will be a work in fruition if you try creating value for people when you don't really know their values and what they really want.

To create value for people, you will need to understand them and what they really need. And to do that you will have to walk in their shoes.

When you have the same shoe size as someone and you wear their shoe, you will understand where their pain points are. If you never try to wear their shoes, you will just be assuming you know their experience with the shoes. And your assumption will lead you to creating the value they don't really want. There are many products in the market that haven't made any headway.

There are opportunities to create value everywhere. When I was working as a teacher in a secondary school. One day in the staff room, I overheard some of the teachers complaining about how the principal, who was busy, had no time to mark his papers thereby delaying the production of results sheet, consequently also delaying their salaries. He set a rule that no teacher will get paid except they have prepared their results sheets.

I didn't judge them or criticize them, I simply gained insight from what they said and used it to create value for the principal. I walked in the shoes of the principal and then created value for him. What was the value I created?

Here are the value I offered him: I said he is a busy man and so,

1. I can help him mark the scripts and record them, or

2. I can record them for him if he has already marked them

This act of generosity on my part really caused him to keep increasing my salary each month till it passed that of other people who were there. He wanted me to be part of his management, unfortunately I had other plans for my life.

Generosity works. But it only works when you are able to understand what someone needs and then come up with what the person wants. Empathy helps you connect with people in a much deeper level. That is why any value that is created from empathy with people resonates with people more.

Don't just assume you know what people need because you don't. You may not even know what you really need let alone what others need. But empathy gives you that.

To walk in other people's shoes means to experience what people are experiencing, to feel what they are feeling, to know what they know and to go through the same thing they are going through.

If you want to create value for people then you need to be touched by the feeling of their infirmity or pain or lack. You need to experience life as they experience it. You need to feel what they are feeling.

Empathy helps you understand and share the feelings of your people to foster deep user understanding and be able to uncover the deep user insights and needs. When you know what they need, it becomes easier to create value they will want.

You have to understand what people are going through and how they are feeling about it to create value for them. Value is not about what you think or feel but what people think and feel. It will only be value because they want it not because you create it. Value is in the eyes of the receiver.

Don't ever assume you know what people really want because you don't

except you choose to first walk in their shoes to know what they really need.

Creating value is solving problems for people. You need to empathize with people to know what exactly their problem is. In solving problems, Empathy helps you do the following:

1. **Understand the problem faced by the people:** You will get to experience the problem without becoming part of the cause of the problem.

2. **Reframe the problem:** When you empathize, you get to know

what the problem is exactly. That way you get to reframe the problem into context.

3. Shape the Solution to the Problem: When the problem get reframed, it becomes easy to begin to shape the solution.

4. Define the Real Need: You will never know the real need of people until you see the world through their eyes and feel what they feel. Their pain may even be the real need and not the problem that you thought. Walking in their shoes will help you uncover that.

5. Understand the People: Empathy aid your understanding of people and why they do the things that they do. Why should you create value for people you don't understand? The secret behind the success of the iPhone is that Steve Jobs understand the people he was creating value for.

6. Speed up Trust: Empathy finds a common ground to connect with people. That fosters trust.

Get to Know The Real Problem

Inability to really understand what the problem really is will lead to a solution that doesn't solve the problem. This has happened many times. A human-right activist was diagnosed with pneumonia and was treated for same. When the sickness got worst, he was taken to the U.K and was diagnosed as having cancer in its advance state. If the first hospital had identified the main problem, they would have prescribed the right solution for it.

Some of the things we call problems are actually symptoms. We need to understand what the real problem is before we can solve it. If not we will just be developing solutions for symptoms instead of the real problem. The problem will never go ahead simply because a solution has been developed for the symptoms. Empathy enables you to pin out the real problem.

The way you define the problem also matters. You have to reframe the problem in a way so that you can to fit the context of the people who are experiencing it.

Consider People's Behaviors In Solving Problems

Empathy also enable you to consider the habits and behaviours (way of life) of the people who are experiencing the problem.

If you develop the value or solution without considering their habits and behaviours, you may end up creating something that completely disrupts their lives. That maybe valuable to you, but not to them.

That was our experience when we went to a community, Buzu community in Northern Nigeria, who had a need for water. We wanted to empower them so they can have a skill with which they can generate income to sustain the water project we did there. We assumed we knew what they needed. We did the market survey and believed there was a need for the candle. So we spent money buying all they needed resources for them to produce candles. We had a vision of a candle factory growing in the midst. We left satisfied that we have done a great job.

Six month after that, they haven't even produced a single candle. The candle making resources remained as we left it. The challenge was that we never considered their way of life when we designed the solution. We were only happy with the idea we had. The project was a failure. It never flew with them.

After empathizing them and observing their way of life, we discovered that they were nomads. So we developed a solution that fitted their way of life. We built a garden for them. They can sell the fruits and earn money. That became value to them and they were able to sustain it.

What You Need to EMPATHIZE

1. You Need to Have a Beginners Mindset

You have to come to the people without any prepared mind. Empty your mind of every prejudice. Come to them with a mind like that of a child. A mind free of any thought about the people. That will help you understand them better.

2. Do not Judge or Criticize

When you judge people or criticize, you will never get anything from them. There is no way you will empathize with people when you are critical of how they do things. The purpose of empathy is to gain insight from understanding the people, their problem and how they relate with it.

If you judge them you have closed up your mind to learn anything about them. It simply means that you have not placed yourself in their shoes.

If you are feeling what they feel, you will understand why they do what they do.

3. Don't Make Assumptions

Most times we make assumptions about what the need of the people are. I did a lot of that until I go to understand that my assumptions are based on my experience and not that of the people. Nokia made assumptions on what kind of phones people need and lose their market share. When Henry Ford was developing the car, there was a particular company that was perfecting the whip for a horse. When Henry Ford produced the car, the company went bankrupt. They assumed what people needed. Even Henry Ford later fell into this assumption and lost market share.

People don't even know what they need. So don't really ask them what they need. Empathize with them and you will gain insight into what they know.

4. Seek First to Understand People

This is one of the habits Stephen Covey wrote about in his book, 7 Habits of Highly Effective People. Before you can offer a solution to people, seek to deeply understand them and their perspective. To understand people, you have to learn to listen and observe.

If you want to be a value giver, it's important to learn to understand people. Don't try to make them understand you or understand their problem, just understand them. Understanding people will lead to understanding their problems and creating value for them.

Just focus your attention on trying to understand people. That alone may even be the value you are adding to them because most people don't understand them.

5. Be Selfless

To succeed with your empathy, you have to focus on them and not seek your own. It's not about you but about them. Focus on them.

You have to be there for them. You have to remove yourself from everything.

Stay focused on their needs and problems and not yours. No matter how much in need you are, forget it. It's not about your needs or what you can get from them but what you can help them do. You can have all your needs met if you will first help them with their problems.

Value Givers understand that in order to have all their needs met, they will need to help other people with their needs. You will only find yourself when you are lost in trying to understand and help other people.

Practice Empathize With People

Empathy is a means to an end and the end is to create value for people.

Whatever you gain from the empathy, you can now use to create value for them. That's the reason for empathy.

1. Find a Common Ground and Connect with People

If you really want to understand people, you have to connect with them. And to connect with them you will have to find a common ground with which to do so.

A common ground is something you and the people are both interested in. That will open the door to their heart. Empathy is built on common interests and values. You have to know what people find valuable and then take interest in it.

As important as this is, most people neglect looking for common ground with people they want to create value for. They make assumptions about what others make like we did. They get so consumed with their agenda rather than focusing on the people and collaborating with them to create value.

It is your responsibility to study them so as to know what this common ground is. It's the place where you guys connect. You have to be deliberate in finding a common ground to connect with the people you want to create value for.

2. Ask Question

The kind of answers you get is determined by the questions asked. If you want to understand things, then ask relevant questions. If you are not asking questions then you are making assumptions. You can only get to know what people are going through when you ask question.

I have discovered that except you are interested in people, you will never ask them question. Really, interest births curiosity. Don't ever ask what the person needs. You will never get the right answer. Instead ask about how the problem came to be and how it affects the person. In those answers, you will get at the root cause of the problem.

People cannot realistically answer that question. You have to ask questions that will reveal their thoughts and feelings or beliefs about the problem.

From understanding the problem, you can reframe it and develop the right solutions. Don't ask what the solution is; they don't that either. You are the Value Giver.

3. Listen Attentively

This is to aid you to hear what is not being said. Most times all we do is listen to what people are saying, but the real secret is in what they are saying without using words. Most of us don't listen to people we only keep quite thinking about what we are going to reply.

You have to hear between the pauses or between the lines. If you want to gain insight into the problem of people, then you have to listen to what they are saying without words.

There are times we want to share things but cannot just put them in words. That's what you should listen for. In those wordless communications lies the insight you need. Empathy requires you to be a good listener and not just a communicator.

4. Observe to See What Eyes Can't See

Observation is deeper than looking. You look but with observation you see with your imagination. You are attentive and watch every little movement.

You have to go where they are and see how they relate with the problem. That will help you understand their culture or way of life. When you observe people, look for patterns in their lives as not relates to the problem.

If you develop a solution that disrupts their way of life, it will not be valuable to them. Observation will not only help you understand their relationship with the problem, but also how the solution you will develop will resonate with them.

You have to know exactly and see how they behave with the problem and solution. That will help you when developing the value. It will help you develop something that fits their lifestyle.

5. Study Their Emotional Attachment to the Problem

Their emotional attachment is based on their beliefs. If you challenge their beliefs they will not connect with you. The more connected emotionally they are with the problem, the harder it is to create a solution that is very disruptive of their lives. Whatever you are building, should consider their emotions and beliefs.

Are they emotionally attached to their problem or not? If they are, the value you are going to create should also shift that attachment to the solution. Trying to change their emotions will lead nowhere. Instead leverage the emotions while developing the value. Wrap their emotions around the value you create.

When you are able to do this, you will gain understanding of the people and will be able to develop the kind of solution that will help you. To create value for people, you need to empathize with them.

CHAPTER SIX

INNOVATE OR LOSE YOUR VALUE

◆ ◆ ◆

T hat you are valuable to people today doesn't mean you are going to always be valuable in the future. We have businesses that were big, rich and great. It was like they will always be around through out eternity. It seemed that they allow that to get into their head and it affected their reasoning. They stopped striving to be better and became like the dinosaurs.

To remain valuable you have to continually innovate your value. What people see as value today, may not be value to them tomorrow. Anyone who wants to remain valuable, need to keep on improving their value.

More than a 100 years ago, Henry Ford innovated in the transportation industry when he created the Model T and mass produced them. He revolutionized transportation thereby disrupting a number of industries including wagon and carriage businesses, and the buggy whip industry. His innovation made them loose value.

Ever since, companies that think they are standing loose market share to those who can innovate. Value is transient. Your value is susceptible to being disrupted if you are not innovating. If you don't innovate, your value dies. It's important that you start, improving your value the moment you deliver it to the users. If you don't, someone elsewhere is working to render it valueless to people by creating something that is much better.

Value Givers are innovators because they solve problems for people and not because they want to make money. Their focus is people and not the money.

They do nothing for money but just to make life easy and better for people. And that is why they are always innovating. They are always following the needs of people and innovating to create value to meet those needs.

The needs of people are always changing. If you solve a problem for people, you will create other problems for them. If you are not solving these new problems, then be sure that someone will get ready to do so in a better way. if you don't find solution to their new problems, you will no longer be relevant to them.

Kodak was into making films for cameras. They invested heavily in making films but then the need of people began to change. Another company noticed this change and started to develop digital photography. Instead of innovating, Kodak didn't because they have invested heavily in the old solution to people's problems. Photography used to be limited by the amount of film you had, but now you can take as much pictures as you want without that limitation. Kodak lost value and had to file for chapter 11 bankruptcy.

Socrates said, "*The secret of change is to focus all your energy, not on fighting the old, but on building the new.*" Innovation brings about change. Whether you react or respond to change will determine how valuable you are. It is better to be either the initiator of the change or to ride on the wave of the change.

Innovation Brings Change

I love the Chinese proverbs that says, "*When the winds of change blow, some people build walls and others build windmills.*" When you innovate, you are changing things and unlocking the value that resides in it. Innovation endows things with new capacity to become valuable.

That you are relevant to your employer today doesn't mean you are going to be relevant all your life except of course if you continually innovate new value. You have to be creating new value to remain relevant and valuable. That is where innovation comes into play.

Innovation is the way value givers create and add value to people and organizations. Anything that will make life easy, beater, and cheaper for people is value to them.

When you innovate you create or come up with better ways to serve people. People want their lives to continually become better.

Apple upgrades its products so that it can remain relevant. They understand that if they think their product is perfect and should not be improved, they will soon become irrelevant. They add new things to it and remove what is not useful so that it can be almost like a new phone. As such people leave the old ones to get the new one. That's because innovation bring about improvement and disruption.

When you improve your value and make it new to meet the new or unfulfilled needs of people, you will be disrupting other value that have been created but never improved to meet this new need.

People want things to continually improve. When you improve through innovation, your service to people will improve and so their lives will get better. They will always seek you out.

You have to focus on the problem of the present and also anticipate the problem of the future. That way you will still be valuable to people. If you never consider the problems of the future, you will be left behind.

If you lose your value, in the same place you were valued, you will be looked down on. People are selfish and only care about what they want. Apple may be revered today, but if it stops meeting the needs of people, it will be avoided like a plague.

It happened to some people in MTN Nigeria. They thought their employer will remember how valuable they were in the past and keep them there. They stopped growing. They stopped improving. Their value became obsolete. They became a drag on the company rather than a plus. Their employer needed new value and not the old. So they lost their jobs.

And I believe they were surprise that they were fired. They have outlived their relevance. Nothing last forever, not even your value. It's easy to give into complacency, believing that one will never be fired because of what they did in the past. The past is gone and you have to create new value to be valuable to your employer.

If a salt loses its value, it's no longer good to be used but to be trample underfoot. So also when you loose your value. You may have been celebrated in the past, but the moment you stop innovating your value, same people who celebrated you will starting calling for your head. They will be the ones shouting "Crucify him!"

Innovation is the process of identifying what people need and creating what they need then finding better ways to add and deliver the value to them. When you innovate you endow resources with the ability to meet the needs of people. Innovators turn things into value for people. Creating things that people needed yesterday and not today is not innovation.

Value Givers add value to things so that it can become valuable and useful to people. They do so as a habit.

Principles of Innovation

1. Innovation Starts with Curiosity

The primary foundation of innovation is curiosity. Without curiosity, individuals and organizations will have a great difficulty in discovering new ideas. Innovation is seeing what everybody has seen, then asking the questions that no one dare ask. Everyone has witnessed an apple falling from a tree, but only Isaac Newton asked the question that brought about the law of gravity. It was an innovation then.

If you are not curious, you will live in a world that doesn't change. Because you will never question or challenge anything. It will remain the same way for you. If you are not asking questions, you will not change anything because you are not changing.

Everyone thought the world was flat but Christopher Columbus questioned that assumption. People believed that if anyone sail off into the distance, they will get to the edge of the world and fall off. Columbus challenged that belief with a question and discovered America. Curiosity as we have come to see is the fuel for discovery, learning and innovation.

Curiosity will keep leading you to new path where you can keep creating value for people. You cannot remain relevant without first asking people question about what is important to them and what they need. You will never be a daring innovator, if you are afraid to question everything. You must kill sacred cows through you question.

We are curious about people because we care. When you care you will notice small changes in what people do and you will take notice. Voltaire said, *"Judge a man by his questions rather than his answers."*

2. Innovation Is the Result of Connections

You need to have ideas if you want to be innovative. The mind cannot have ideas without reading. This means that to have ideas, you have to read books in that area or study other fields. Innovation is all about connecting ideas.

In truth there is nothing really new. Everything is just a copy of something that already exist, which is then added to something. You cannot innovate anything for people without first having ideas and then connecting them. You can innovate by associating different products from a different industry to create something people can find useful.

Steve Jobs, co-founder of Apple, said, *"Creativity is just connecting things. When you ask creative people how they did something, they feel a little guilty because they didn't really do it, they just saw something. It seemed obvious to them after a while."* Connecting an idea from one field or industry to another can result in innovation.

The most important characteristic of an idea is not its ability to create but to be valuable to people. Ideas have to be converted into something useful to be seen as innovation. connecting ideas make them useful.

3. Innovation has to Be Useful to People

Most people have ideas, great ones at that, but they are just ideas and cannot be of value to people.

Take for instance, I have an idea on how to generate electric energy from sound. It's just an idea and has no value to people. When it becomes useful to people, then it is called innovation.

Do you know how many people have the idea for Facebook? But only Mark Zukerberg turned it into value for everyone. People have an idea of electric cars, but only Elon Musk turned that idea into an innovation. Ideas are a dime a dozen, but turning them to something valuable to people is where the real work lies.

The bridge between idea and innovation is work. You have to work to turn the idea into something useful. What you work will work and be useful to people. When you do that you become valuable.

4. The Speed at Which You Innovate Determines Your Relevance and Value

What we are doing now is quite different from what we were doing last year. As we innovate, we get better and more valuable. Innovation make you bring more value to the marketplace.

If you are doing what you were doing years back today, no one will want to associate with you. I believe no one will want to do business with a company that uses a manual type writer for all its word processing work today.

The person who is fast at innovating will steal the market from the slow. Speed is a great competitive advantage when it comes to value creation and delivery. How fast you can create value for people, will determine how relevant you will be.

Anyone who is slow in innovating will become old school and obsolete, just occupying space. Some people stop working on new value the moment they graduate from school. We are in a world were speed of innovation counts a lot.

Value givers know that their value is tied to what they do to people and not just what they get. How fast they can detect the needs of people and respond to it with an innovative solution will determine their relevance.

How fast you come up with solutions for people's problems will determine how relevant you are.

5. Your Growth without Innovation is not Valuable

It is good to grow. It's great to read books and listen to audio programs. It's exciting to be learning new things. But if what you are learning is not making you create things that are useful to people, then you are not becoming valuable.

If all your efforts and growth doesn't translate to innovation for people, it's a waste of time. That was my challenge years back. I thought growth is just about me. I read lots of book. Instead of being humble, I became prideful. What I learned should have made me useful to people, but it didn't. It took time but I gradually changed.

You don't grow for yourself but rather you grow so that you can add value to people. If your growth doesn't become innovation, then it's a waste and has no relevance.

6. Innovation Improves The Lives of People

If what you are doing only improves your life and not that of others, then you are not innovating. My life began to get better and improve when I started innovating for people to improve their lives.

We all have our lives but it's not for us but for people. We live for people. If you are doing nothing to make life better for people, you are not improving.

Your life should be lived to make life better for others. When improving the lives of people becomes your focus, innovation will come easy for you. Ideas will come easily to you because you want to make life better for people.

7. Mistakes Can Become Innovations

Mistakes are not bad on their own. If you are not trying anything new, you will never make a mistake. Mistakes are made when we step out of our comfort zone.

But the mistakes you make in life can become the innovation that will help many other people in life. The lessons you learned from the mistake you make can become valuable to someone. Evaluated experience can become valuable and profitable to someone. Mistakes and failures are good. Don't throw them away. Milk them for the value you can get from them. There are gems to innovate from them. If you keep looking, you will find something in them that is valuable to people.

8. To Innovate You Have to Focus on The User

If your focus is on yourself you will never innovate. You have to focus on people. People are the object of innovation. If what you are doing is not aimed at making life better for people, you will never innovate.

If an employer is overly concerned about himself, he will never do anything to make his work better, thereby adding value to his colleagues and employer. No one can be self-centered and be innovative.

Attend to the state of the people and know their needs, then focus on making life easy for them and you will always be valuable to them. It's about them and not just you.

9. Innovation is a Process

Innovation is a process not an event or an idea you come up with at once. There were times when I wished I could just come up with innovative ideas just like that. But even an event takes time to plan. The planning process of an event is what really makes the event possible and successful. Making life better for people is a process and not a one time thing.

Isaac Newton didn't just noticed an apple falling down from a tree and came up with the idea of gravity. He must have been working on that idea for something. He noticed it because he programmed his mind to see in that area.

Innovation is a mindset. If your mindset is not programmed to see things, you will never see them. Innovation don't just pop up like pop corn, it takes time. During those times, the mind is being programmed to think, associate and connect ideas. What people do daily and intentionally over time results in innovation.

Innovation is created daily, not in a day. Innovation is a lot like investing successfully in the stock market. If your desire is to create an innovation in a day, then, you are not going to be successful. The goal of anyone who wants to innovate should be to get a little better each day and to build on the previous day's and other people's work.

If you are getting better each day, you have a more chance of innovating. The person who is not improving, cannot innovate.

10. Innovation Comes Through Inspiration

Innovation is anything that adds value to people. People become innovative when they are passionate about things. If you are not passionate, you will not be inspired. Inspiration is listening to your inner voice. Inspiration must be based on your empathy and observing of people. The insight, inspiration, you gain will help you innovate.

The challenge with most people is that they think that innovative ideas just fall on people who are not prepared, who have not given it much studies and thoughts.

When you are mentally stimulated about something you are passionate about, you will easily come up with ideas on what to do to make it better. It is a feeling of enthusiasm when you are doing something you are passionate about. Enthusiasm means to be filled with God. When you are filled with God, you get inspired with ideas.

Paulo Coelho, the author of The Alchemist, said, *"When we love, we always strive to become better than we are. When we strive to become better than we are, everything around us becomes better too."* Whatever you are passionate about, you will be inspired to make better. If you love people, you will easily get inspired to make life better for them by adding value to them.

Innovate Your Value

The following are the ways you can innovate your value

1. Addition

Here you add to something and make it easy and faster for the people. Ask yourself the question: what can I add to make this thing valuable to people?

You can combine old things and come up with something new that is useful to people.

Apple did that by combining an MP3 player, Internet browser, apps, email and a phone together on one device to form something new and useful called the iPhone which has made them very valuable. This has made life better for people.

When you combine ideas, you will come up with something new that will add value to people. To be able to do that, you have to be a T: have deep knowledge in one of two fields and shallow knowledge in many other fields. A knowledge in one field combined with knowledge in another field will result in something that will be valuable to people. Innovation comes through addition.

2. Adopt to Adapt

You can borrow something from one industry and bring it to work where you are or for people. Innovators are like great artists: they borrow or steal from the work of others to make something new as Steve Jobs put it, "Good artists copy, great artists steal." When the work of others inspire you, you can find uses for that same idea in another field to create value for people.

There is nothing new under the sun. Everything you see and use are all gotten from something that already exist. Borrowing ideas is using an existing idea or concept as the resource to create a new value for people.

Take for instance, human's borrowed the idea of how a chicken hatch an egg to create business incubators. Sometimes the ideas you need to innovate value will come from outside your field or setting. You will have to borrow or steal the idea from outside and adapt it to what you are doing.

You can borrow things from anywhere then adapt it to create what will help people have a better and easy life.

3. Subtract From Something

Innovation happens when you remove a part of something that is not contributing to what people really need. That makes life simpler and easier for people. Apple removed all the buttons you don't need on the phone to make it easy for people. Rather than have the keyboard even when you don't need, they removed it so it can only appear when you do need it.

You can innovate value by taking away anything that doesn't directly contribute to what people really use it for. You have to put yourself in people's shoes to understand how they interact with the value that is out there, which you want to innovate.

If anything is distracting them from using it, then it's not simple. Albert Eisntein said, *"When the solution is simple, God is answering."* To make it simple you have to subtracting what distracts in order to enhance what is useful and essential.

You need to ask this question: what can you take away from what already exist to make it more simpler and easier to use? Simplicity is the ultimate sophistication we are told. You can create value by making things simpler.

4. Multiply Something

When you find something that works for people and they really like it, you can multiply its effect and work. Find out the one single part of the value you created that people find useful and enhance it. You can enhance by subtracting what distracts from the essential or by multiplying the essential.

If I find a particular program we teach has great impact on people and people like it, I will multiply it and do it more. I will enhance it and make it more impactful. That's innovation.

This means you will increase what works or people find useful. If I do something to my employer and it brings value to him, I will multiply that so that people will find it more useful.

To multiply means to differentiate and scale.

Ask the question: what can you do to differentiate your value or approach. You have to make it different from what others are doing so you can scale it to a level that is different.

CHAPTER SEVEN

INCREASE YOUR INFLUENCE

◆ ◆ ◆

Value Givers are influential people. Anyone who consistently create and add value to people will become influential. We all respond to people who add value to us, but react to those who take value and try to manipulate us.

It's like this. You open yourself to someone who give to you but close yourself up from anyone who you know always takes from you. We all love people who are always adding value to us.

If you increase your value to people, you are basically increasing your influence with them. Anything you do that increases your value, also increases your influence. Just keep doing it and you will become highly influential.

If you want to make any meaning or difference in life, you will need to become valuable. If you want to be influential, focus on creating what will help people and they will allow you to influence them.

A life is not meaningful except it influences people to be more than they are. Impact is a result of influence. The way to influence is to be a person who constantly create and give value to people.

When you are giving value, you may think that you are not influential but one day it will all compound. Small seemingly insignificant consistent value addition to people will over time produce massive influence.

I send out my blog post. Someone who is a pastor even blocked me. I never allowed that to bother me. I remained stedfast and consistent in adding value to people. Then one day, someone told me what he read and how it made him to start thinking. He called his wife and discussed it with her. It was a write up about making money while you sleep. It changed the way they think and what they were doing. I have influenced him and his wife through that article.

Only God knows how many people are being influenced by those write ups. If you continually give value to people soon you will have momentum and the compounded effect of the value you sent out will be massive. The way of the Value Giver is the way of influence.

Whatever you give is what you own and it will definitely come back to you in multiplied form. People who only take from others are only out to manipulate them.

Bill Gates Was Influenced To Influence the World

Every influencer had someone who saw value in them and influenced them to be what they are. Bill Gates, who arguably, has influenced the world we live in, had his life changed when he was in 4th grade by a woman who he will later thank personally for positively influencing his life.

In 4th grade, Bill was a typical introverted nerd who love read books. He always did his best to be alone, keeping himself to himself. But then a Value Giver named Blanche Caffiere, happened upon the scene of his life and influenced him to influence the world.

Bill Gates wrote about her influence in his blog. He wrote:

"When I fiesta met Mrs Caffiere, she was the elegant and engaging school librarian at Seattle's View Ridge Elementary, and I was a timid fourth grader. I was desperately trying to go unnoticed, because I had some big deficits, like atrocious handwriting… and I was trying to hide the fact that I liked to read- something that was cool for girls but not for boys… Mrs Caffiere took me under her wing and helped make it okay

for me to be a messy, nerdy boy who was reading lots of books."
She influenced him by adding value to him. She listened to him, encouraged him to pursue his passion for reading and challenged him by questioning what he had learned. Her influence gave him confidence. We may not have known of Bill Gates today if that woman had not appeared in his life and influenced him.

Principles of Influence

1. Influence Starts With Your Growth

The more you grow, the more valuable you become. So as you grow so does your influence increases. If you want to become more influential with people, then invest in your personal growth. To double your influence, triple your investment in the expansion of your capacity and increase of your capability. The more you are able to do, the more influence you can wield.

2. You have to be You to be Influential

There is no way you can be influential if you are not authentic. You have to be yourself. The value you produce must come from inside you not you being a copy of someone. Be true to yourself to create the kind of value that will influence people.

If I quote someone, it's the person influencing people not me. To influence people, I have to be me and my value need to be unique. There is no way you will influence others when you are not you. Your influence is a fruit of who you are.

3. Consistency Makes You Influential

Most of us think that the moment you start adding value to people you become influential. Becoming influential takes time. You have to build trust with people to influence them.

You have to be consistent and relentless. Someone posted 45 blog posts before he was noticed. It's easier to give up before you get anywhere. The marketplace is crowded, so you need to put in more effort for a longer time to breakthrough the noise and be able to influence people.

Focusing on the big picture helps you stick to the process. If you are not focused on the big picture, you will give up when you are closer to being influential. You have to be consist in doing what you are doing to become influential.

4. You Have to Convince You Before You Can Influence Others

If you cannot convince yourself of something, there is no way you can influence people. Your convictions will make you influential. Whatever you are not convinced of, you can never influence people with. Whatever moves you, you can use to move people.

Anyone who is influencing the world, even in death, is someone who was fully persuaded about something and totally sold out to it.

When you are fully persuaded about a thing, it is easier to influence people in that area. You will never influence people when you have not fully given yourself to a cause or idea. Value Givers are sold out to the value they are creating. They believe in it and are ready to give it all that it takes.

5. When You Earn Trust, Doors Open to Influence

No one will trust you when you just do something once and give you. You have to continually add value to become influential. You have to stay in there. It is the person who stays in that people trust.

I started adding value to people a few years back on my birthday and today my influence is increasing because of that. My influence grew because the people trusted me. I have demonstrated to them that I can keep my word and that I was doing it not for what I can get from them but just to make them better and life better for them.

People are skeptical of anyone who is not ready to give but wants to take. There is no way you can get when you have not sown anything. Trust is reaped. You have to build trust with people. They have to trust you first before you can influence them.

6. When the Good of People is Your Priority, You Will be Top on Their Influential People Scale

You have to make seeking the good of people your topmost priority to influence them. If you are focused only on yourself, you will be manipulative. Influence is always about seeking the good of people. They must give you permission to influence them.

Marriages have challenges when the couples begin to seek their own and not make the needs of their spouse their top priority.

If you focus only on what you get, you will become emotionally manipulative instead of influential. If you make the needs of your spouse your priority, your spouse will give you permission to influence him or her.

7. Your Influence Develop Daily and not in a Day

Influence development is a process. It takes time. I used to think that I can become influential overnight. Yes, you can be influential overnight. But that night will take 10 years or more. It is really one of the longest nights you will ever have. You have to also be doing the same thing through out those nights.

You have to go deeper to build your influence. If you don't go deeper, you will never become influential for long. Your influence should not be like that of the mushroom, which has no root. It pop up one minute and then next it is gone. Take time to build your root downwards so that you can grow your influence upward.

Of course, you can influence people based on your position and relationship with them, but the best kind of influence that makes the world a better place takes time. It is is based growing yourself, so that you can influence others to grow. Growing people influence others to become better.

Some people are just as influential as the mushroom. They influence for a moment and the next moment, they are no longer influential. To be perpetually influential, you will need to go through the process.

Processes of Influence

People don't become influential overnight, they are only noticed overnight. Influence is built over the years. Consistency builds influence in the following ways;

- Commit To Growing Daily
- Master Your Emotions
- Practice Your Craft To Improve
- Consistency to Generate Momentum
- Take Baby Steps in Giving Value
- Build The Right Beliefs and Habits

- Do What You Say

Increasing Your Influence

The benefit of being an influencer are numerous. You can get endorsement deal, companies will want you on their products and boards and so on. It pays to pay the price and become a influential person.

Do the following and you will be influential

1. Become an Expert or Authority

You are not creating and adding value when you just copy what someone said or share video with people. That person is the one influencing others. I have never heard of someone who became authority in sharing what others do.

A preacher embellished his speaking with quotes of what others said. He was only trying to impress people with knowledge and not add value to them. People came to listen to what he has to say to make their lives better and not to hear what someone or that person said. It is not bad to quote others, but you need to use it explain your point and to add value to people.

It is what comes out of you that influences the world. It is what you craft on your inside that will change the world and not what anyone says. What the other person said influenced you, so what you will say will influence others.

You have to become an expert on your chosen field. Bill Gates is an influencer not because he is rich but because he is an expert in building a business. It took him time to become an expert. Steve Jobs influenced the world because he became an expert in design and marketing over time.

When you become an expert you are an authority on something and when you speak people tend to listen. People listen to people who have influence. When influential people speaks or do something, people pay attention.

In Nigeria everyone is an expert. Someone reads a book and becomes an expert over night. It is the reason why the level of manipulation is high. There is no way you can influence people when you are not genuinely an expert who has practiced and experienced what you are teaching or saying. What you say must be part of your life to be influential.

It takes like 7 to 10 years being on the same thing to be an expert so that when you talk, everyone listens. Most people are in a hurry so they have no time to spend learning and practicing their craft to become authorities in it. Through deliberate practice, you improve your craft till you become an expert.

2. Go Above & Beyond

You need to set a standard for the value you give. People should associate you with something that is hard to find. You should be excellent. You should be exceptional. You should always be on the extra mile where there is no traffic jam.

Raise the bar of what you give to people so that it gets difficult to copy you. Let it not be substandard. Even if you start with that, you have to make sure that you continue to improve on that. When people begin to copy you, you will come up with something far better. You just keep drawing a circle around them.

If you keep improving, your value will keep increasing. Look at Apple. The first iPhone had glitches but today, many iPhones and improvements after, they are the best and everyone is being influenced by them. They are the leaders in smartphone. Everyone looks to them. They influence every smartphone company.

They are so influential that their net worth is in trillions of dollars. Influence comes with money. See ahead to stay ahead. If you are the one who always define the reality, you will be influential.

3. Give More Than is Expected

For a number of years now, I have been sending books to corporate organizations in Nigeria and abroad. I am giving them what they don't expect to get. I have not received any response from my giving, but I know that one day, the fruits of the giving will come in.

In 2018, we spent millions of naira sending out books, giving them more value. The influence that will result will greatly compensate for all the effort and resources so far expended to add value to them.

Why do I do that? I cannot teach you this program if I have not practiced it

It is called having integrity. I teach what I have experience not what I read. That's why it carries life and power to influence. Most people are not generous. They are waiting for others to be generous to them.

We are living in a time when greed is rampant and people are out to take and not to give. Even when they give, it's never much. To standout and stand head taller than everyone, you need to go the extra mile in your giving.

An employee who always do and go beyond what is expected of her in the workplace will become more influential in the workplace. If you do what you are being paid to do, you will never be able to influence anyone. But when you develop the habit of doing more than you are paid to do, influence become the perfume you wear. Doing more than you are paid to do is an investment in your future.

Doing more than is expected of you, going above and beyond, is a culture that becomes a strategic advantage for businesses. Customers are looking for companies that will wow them by doing far more than they are compensated for. That way you will beat competitors. When you are in the habit of doing more for your customers, you will not have to worry about your competitors.

4. Listen and Connect

To connect you have to focus on people and believe in them. You can never become influential if you don't listen to them. Everyone really like the sound of their voice. We want to speak so that others will listen. We assume that we are influential when we speak, but the truth is that we are more influential when we listen to people.

When we get feedback from our clients about what we are doing, we quickly do to correct it. When people know that you always heed their corrections, you connect with them and can influence them. But when a business continually ignores their customers feedback, the day of their influence has come to an end.

You have to go beyond their mind and touch their hearts if you want to be influential. Listen to what people are saying and you will connect to them. Don't pretend you are listening when you all the while thinking only about what you are going to say. Make sure your whole being is concentrated on listening and hearing them.

You become more influential when you listen to people than when they listen to you. When you listen to them, they develop trust with you. They feel a sense of connectedness with you. That opens them up to your influence. The truth is that if you listen to them, you can influence them.

5. Be Gracious and Appreciative

When you criticize and judge people, you will never influence them. I have experienced that. Surprisingly, we assume that the more we bully people with criticism, the more they will give us permission to influence them. Human nature doesn't allow that. Be gracious to people instead of being judgmental.

A woman who always speak against her kids or husband, never gracious and appreciative is hard to really influence them. You have to genuinely become appreciative of the little efforts people expend to make things happen.

When you appreciate and encourage people and speak good words to them, you will influence them. You will be more influential when you use honey with people than when you use vinegar. The words you speak to people should be encouraging to build them up rather than discouraging to tear them down.

Saying "Thank you" and meaning it can go a long way in making you influential. It has never taken anything from anyone. But some are just unable to really say they are grateful. They are afraid of being influenced. Possibly someone has used that to manipulate them. So they are being careful.

Being appreciative builds your influence.

6. Demonstrate Care by Solve Their Problems

If you are not interested in what people are going through and how you can help them come out of it, you will not be influential. People don't really care what you know, but they do care when you demonstrate you care for them. To care for people is to help them solve their problems and meet their needs.

CHAPTER EIGHT

BECOME A DOMINATOR

◆ ◆ ◆

Value Givers are not jack of all trades; they are T. They are specialists in a field but with shallow knowledge in other fields. That gives them great advantage. Their goal in every field they are in is to dominate it. They have to own it and then dominate it.

Joaquín "El Chapo" Guzmán became Mexico's top drug kingpin in 2003. Each year from 2009 to 2011, Forbes magazine ranked Guzmán as one of the most powerful people in the world, ranking him 41st, 60th, and 55th, respectively.

He was thus the second most powerful man in Mexico, after Carlos Slim. The magazine also calls him the "biggest drug lord of all time."

The U.S. federal government considers Guzmán "the most ruthless, dangerous, and feared man on the planet" and the Drug Enforcement Administration (DEA) estimated that he matched the influence and reach of Pablo Escobar and considered him "the godfather of the drug world".

In 2013, the Chicago Crime Commission named Guzmán "Public Enemy Number One" for the influence of his criminal network in Chicago, though there is no evidence that he has ever been in that city.

The last person to receive such notoriety was Al Capone in 1930. What in hell could you personally have in common with the biggest drug lord of all time?

He is simply a dominator. His story will illustrate this.

As the tale goes, back when El Chapo was a soldier who served and took orders from the big boss in one of the Mexican cartels, he figured out a way to get drugs from Columbia into the U.S. via digging a tunnel that went under the border.

When he went to the big boss and told him the tunnel was done and that he could move several tons of cocaine if the boss would put him in contact with the reigning drug lord, Pablo Escobar, the boss told him that he was biting off more than he could chew.

He told Chapo they already had a guy handling the cocaine, to give up on the idea and just stick with moving marijuana.

El Chapo refused to let this opportunity pass him by. He knew that cocaine was far more profitable and the more of it they could move, the better it would be for their cartel.

He had a friend in Pablo's organization that he reached out to asking him to introduce him to Pablo, which he agrees to do.

Upon meeting for the first time, Pablo ignores El Chapo's attempt to shake his hand and the first words that come out of his mouth are, "Look you son of a bitch, Barranquillero (the guy who set up the meeting and vouched for him) may trust you, but I don't. Do something that feels off, and I'll kill you, son of a bitch."

Hardly the warm welcome he was hoping for.

Chapo had to start off by admitting that the big boss didn't send him and that he came on his own account.

Escobar saw this as him having balls and said, "Tell me quickly. I don't have time. We're getting tired of Amado's late deliveries. You're saying you can deliver faster?"

He told Pablo that instead of 5 days, he could deliver in 3 days.

Pablo scoffs at this saying, "If he wants, he can do that too. He's just too damn lazy."

And sensing that Chapo had shot his load and was offering nothing enticing, Pablo told his sponsor to get him the fuck out of his face. Time's up.

Less than 30 seconds into having an audience with Escobar, Chapo's chance is slipping away and out of desperation he tells Pablo he can get the drugs across the border and deliver it in 48 hours.

This promise gets Pablo's attention. Pablo says, "Chapo, do you know what happens to those who fail me?"

He confirmed he did.

Pablo says, "So, you can deliver one ton in 48 hours? Prove it and we can start talking business."

He did and the rest is history. It was the drug-smuggling equivalent of Bannister running the 4-Minute Mile. Once Pablo had this miracle performed and Chapo showed up to the boss with the brief cases of cash made from this transaction, neither side could ignore the reality Chapo had opened their eyes to.

Chapo wasn't satisfied with being average. He wanted more. He was discontented with normal. He stretched and did what people thought was impossible and dominated the business. This may not be a good example of a Value Giver, but the principles behind it are.

Dominate Markets

This particular chapter reminds me of a book I wrote, *Compete Like Apple*.

In it I explained how Apple goes for domination and not just to own market shares and they do it so well.

If you are not out to dominate where you are, you are simply not doing enough. If you have other people who you look up to in the field where you are, you are not dominating.

Value givers dominate by using the value they are creating. But first, they have to dominate themselves. Thats where domination starts. If you cannot dominate yourself, you will never be able to dominate anyone.

When you dominate, you become a monopoly.

That was the secret of John D. Rockefeller. He understood the dominion concept of the Value Giver. He swallowed up competitors in every business he entered, created demand by generosity and delivered massive value to people.

When he entered China to sell Kerosene to the people there. He discovered that they don't use kerosene lamps, so he bought a lot of lamps and gave it for free, thereby creating demand for his product. He literally dominated the market he created. You too can do the same.

When we started Millionaire Maker, there was no demand for what we were doing, but now we are creating the demand and dominating the market. You have to go beyond the norm if you want to dominate. If you know what others are doing, then do more than they do.

When you dominate, you monopolize everything, you become the David who slayed Goliath and dominated the field. You become the reigning king of the field or industry that you dominated.

Advantages of Being a Monopoly

1. You Control the field

You become the person who leads the field. When you sneeze everyone catches a cold. You are in charge of that field. You set the rules of engagement and operations. Everyone looks up to you and want to be like you.

It's great to really be in charge. What is the essence of playing catch up when you can be in charge?

2. You determine the Price

People who dominate are the ones who determine the price they charge not the people. As a monopoly, they are the only one providing the product or services they are providing. They can chose any price and people will willingly buy from them.

If you are following others, they will determine the price while you do catch up to get the crumbs. Monopolies take majority of the money available in a market.

3. They charge high price

You may start with a small price for your product or services but as soon as you dominate and monopolize the field, you can start charging a high amount. Take Apple for instance, they enter into markets they can dominate. They don't have competitors. So they can afford to charge a premium for their products.

If you become an expert in your field who provide unique service to people and have dominated the market, you can afford to charge a premium for your services. You are the leader of the field. At this point there is no one people can go to. People who create exceptional value are monopolies and charge high fees.

4. Provide Exceptionally Unique Value

Monopolies provide unique value that are exceptional. What they provide is way different from what anyone provides. They understand that if what they provide can be gotten anywhere else, they are no longer a monopoly. They put in great effort to differentiate what they do from the pack and make it exceptional.

They do so by building brands and not commodities. Psychologically people don't really see commodities as being unique and having exceptional value. As such they buy based on the price rather than value. People buy brands based on the perceived value. To many brands are unique, exceptional and stand for something.

If you want to be a monopoly, then make sure you are building brands and not commodities.

5. Set High Standard

They set high standard that makes it difficult for anyone to join their field.

Because of the standard that they set everyone is afraid to join them. The standard is set around the product they produce, the service they render and how they always do more than the promise. Doing so gives them the monopolistic advantage.

If you do what everyone does, you will make it easy for anyone who wants to join the field or industry you are in. But when the standard of performance is high and it's set by you, then you will enjoy the benefit of being a monopoly.

Being a dominator is not about not having competitors but about doing things in such a way that it becomes hard for competitors to copy you or even do what you are doing.

You have to also make sure that you are constantly breaking the standards you set and create new higher ones.

6. Be Well Positioned in the Mind of People

People and businesses who are dominators make sure that they are well positioned in the mind and heart of people. They understand that being a dominator is all about perception. So they focus on changing the perception of people to see them as the only people who can provide the kind of service that they desire. As Evan Carmichael puts it, when he said, *"Whenever they think of what you do, you should be the first person who comes to mind."*

They own a word in the heart of people. Whenever people hear the word, they associate and attribute that word to them. To be a dominator, you have to use a word or attribute to position yourself in the mind of the people. The battle of dominion doesn't happen in the field but in the mind of people.

Whatever people continually hear you say and see you do, they associate you with. You need to find one word that will represent who you are. Google has become a word that stands for searching the Internet because they have dominated that field. Facebook stands for social media. When you dominate, your name become the word people use to represent what you do.

As a Value Giver, you can and should monopolize the area that you are producing value.

To Become a Monopoly, do the Following;

1. Know the Changing Needs of People You Want To Serve

The needs of people are ever changing. You have to find their needs and then fill it.

2. Meet an Unmet Needs

There are needs that no one is meeting, find those needs and then meet them.

3. Kill Your Value to Create a New One

If you stay with an old value many people will copy it and then catch up with you. So you have to deliberately kill the value you have to create a new one so that you can stay ahead of the pack.

4. Become 10x Better Than Anyone With What You Create

To be a monopoly you have to become better than every one in that field. You have to give them a very wide gap that they cannot catch up with. You have to constantly keep getting better.

Some years back I told myself that I want to be 10 years ahead of people in my field and 10 times better than them. Thats a wide gap. This made me to start doing things that most of them don't do. I started spending more money on my personal growth and building on my capability than they did. I read 10 times more than they do and think and create ten times more value than they do.

Before most people will get to where I am and how I think, I am 10 years ahead. That keeps me dominating the field for 10 years at least. As I do this consistently, I began to enjoy the power of compounded effect. I have noticed that it takes some people 10 years to understand what I said 10 years ago.

5. Give More Value Than Anyone Will Dare

We are creating a monopoly by giving massive value to anyone who either buys our books or get into our programs. We are constantly looking for ways to give more to people than we receive in payment. We give more than anyone in our field.

We are out to dominate and not to play safe. This was what Grant Cardone did. He knew the challenge he had was that no one really knew him, so he decided to give more value than anyone gives so that he can dominate the sales field. He wants to be known as the Godfather of Sales. He started by instructing his team to gather enough content to post every six minutes on the social media for a total of one hundred unique tweets a day. That way he took his expertise in sales and became the dominate brand in sales.

Most people are hoarders, but we are givers. And the word of wisdom of King Solomon never fails. He said the generous soul shall be made rich. That is, the world of the generous will continually keep expanding until he becomes the most dominant.

When you continually give value, you are going to end up dominating your field and everyone will get to know you.

6. Satisfy and Wow The People You Serve

It is not enough to just give value, you have to ensure that it satisfies and wow people. I wish someone had taught me this many years back. I would have used it to dominate the workplace.

So make sure as you provide value for people even if it is for free that you are satisfying them and wowing them. To wow people you have got to do the things they never expect that you were going to do for them. Meet your promises and then meet their other needs that they never expected you are going to meet.

You will wow people by the experience that you create. If you create the right experience, it will amaze them.

How To Be a Dominator

To be able to dominate in every industry, I came up with a list of things you have to commit to do consistently. They are listed below.

- Know What People Need.
- Create a Perception That Only You Can Meet Their Needs.
- Link Your Value to a Cause.
- Keep Improving Your Value.
- Develop Competence To Meet Needs No One Can.
- Make Everything You Do to Meet Their Needs 10x better.
- Do What No One Else is Doing & Willing to Do.

Processes of Dominating

When God created us He created us to live in dominion. That is for us to dominate whatever and wherever we are. We are not to dominate people but to dominate things and make them valuable. If you are not bringing value out of things and using it to serve people, then you are not living in dominion.

If you are not dominating in your field then you are not living from who you really are. That's your authentic self. If you are doing what everyone else is doing, you will never dominate. You are simply repeating or copying what someone has already done.

You are not created to copy anyone but rather to create unique value that the world have not seen. You are created unique and different. The way you think and see the world is different from others. You need, therefore, to leverage your uniqueness to bring unique value to people.

When you are living in dominion, then you will really be making a difference in the lives of people. Live in such a way that you will be contributing your uniqueness as value to people. You are on earth to serve someone with value. I believe each one of us is sent to the earth by God to make life better for humanity. That is what living is.

1. Be Fruitful- Create Value

We, humans, have this special ability among all living things to be creators of value. The proof that we are really living is when we are using our mind to create value for people. Just as a tree can only bear fruit when it grows, so also we can only create value when we expand our mind.

Dominating starts from creating value that is unique to you. If you copy peoples' values, you will never dominate. It must be unique to you. The only way you can find and connect to your uniqueness is if you grow.

2. Multiply Your Value

You are to duplicate and scale the value you created. Take for instance, Madonna produce one master of her album and then she make copies from that master. That is multiplying.

You can only replenish and subdue when you multiply it. Most people just stay in the be fruitful stage. If you create a value that you cannot scale or multiply, you will never dominate.

3. Replenish - Fill Needs

You can now use what you have created to meet the needs of people. The more people whose needs you meet, the more your dominion. To replenish you have to find a way to distribute your value so you can reach as many people as possible. The value you created must dominate the needs of the people.

Apple, Coca Cola, Microsoft and so on are filling needs with the value they created and multiplied and they are dominating because the value is authentic and unique to them and is dominating the needs of people.

4. Subdue All Needs

One you have successfully dominated the need in people's lives, then begin to look for ways to dominate all other needs in their lives. The value you first created was to get their attention, the next thing to do is to create experiences around your values that will meet their other needs.

Microsoft started with operating system and then ventured into application software and many more just to meet the needs of people. Apple started with computers but eventually ventured into MP3 players, music, books, phones, apps, TVs, watch and so on. They began to meet adjacent needs.

If they don't do that, someone can launch an attack on their position by going in to meet adjacent needs.

This was the strategy Tecno used to enter the Nigerian phone market. They came in meeting the needs of people who want to buy cheap phones. At the time when they came in, Nokia and Samsung phones were quite expensive for the average Nigerian to buy. As Tecno began to gain trust and dominate the cheap phone market, the began to create phones for the high end market, launching an attack at the position of Nokia and Samsung. And they succeeded.

To protect your position as a monopoly, don't just focus on one need of your customers. Develop value that will meet many other needs they have. When you fortify yourself as the dominating brand who meets one of their needs, launch another value that will meet other needs. That way you are subduing their needs.

If you follow this process well, you will live in dominion. You will dominate every filled or industry that you enter into.

CHAPTER NINE

OBSESSED WITH MAKING IMPACT

◆ ◆ ◆

T o be obsessed is to be crazy over something. You love it so much that you don't want to give it up. Crazy people are the ones who make things happen.

No one ever make any difference in life or with people without first becoming obsessed about making the impact.

Obsession is being unreasonable. If people understand you, you are not obsessed. I am yet to see a place where people understand someone who is obsessed with a cause or goal. They are unreasonable and they make things happen. They are just not understood. They are termed crazy.

People who are obsessed with making impact are the ones who end up doing so. George Bernard Shaw said, *"The reasonable man adapts himself to the world: the unreasonable one persists in trying to adapt the world to himself. Therefore, all progress depends on the unreasonable man."* Reasonable people are not passionate about anything. They just do things for the sake of it.

Reasonable people do things for the money while the unreasonable do it for their passion. They put their whole life into it. They don't go half measure; they either are in or out. Reasonable people wait for others to initiate things before they take steps, the unreasonable do it anyway.

That's how Value Givers are. If you are not obsessed with making impact in life, you will never make impact. When challenges come you will give up. I have seen many people start with so much passion until something happens, then they forget all about what they said and abandon what they were doing.

Value Givers stick to what they do. No matter how hard it gets, they stay there because they know it makes them better. Tough situations only make them better. They are relentless.

You need to know that there is no such thing as a part time obsession. Some people are only obsessed when things are going in their favor. That is not obsession. You have to be obsessed all the time.

Until you become obsessed with what you are doing, no one will really take you seriously. You have to be fanatical about your mission and why. If you want to create value to impact lives, then you have to become obsessed with that. It means you have to do everything for it.

When you are obsessed with something, every part of you gets involve. You are sold out to it. You will make what you are obsessed work. I have found this to be true in my life. What I am never obsessed with, I leave it the way it is. But being obsessed pushes me to make things happened.

I have been obsessed with improving science and engineering education and application in Nigeria right from when I was 20 years old. I have held on to this dream for more than twenty years now. The journey has been tough, but I have weathered it.

When we had a partnership with Chevron and they decided to do what they wanted to do rather than what we agreed on, I had to end the partnership. I remember them saying I was going to destroy the organization I started. The truth is we were getting money from them and they had good plans for us. I decided we need to follow our obsession rather than someone else's desire. I was never understood for my decision.

When you are obsessed you will do anything and go outside your comfort zone to impact people. You will posses the "whatever it takes" attitude. Here is what being obsessed with what you are doing means:

It is like Steve Jobs shouting at his team at three in the morning about a project delay.

It is Bill Gates sleeping on the floor of his office, rather than take the trouble of going home during the early days of Microsoft.

It is Mother Teresa helping the poor when she could have been doing something else.

It is Thomas Edison persevering when he tried 10,000 times before finally inventing the commercially viable light bulb.

It is Abraham Lincoln enduring failure after failure till he was elected the President of United States of America.

Value Givers are obsessed with the impact they want to make in the world. If you are not obsessed you won't make much impact. People who have made the world better are people who are obsessed with what they are doing. As Steve Jobs said about them, "You can quote them, disagree with them, glorify or vilify them, but the only thing you can't do is ignore them because they change things... They push the human race forward, and while some may see them as the crazy ones, we see genius, because the people who are crazy enough to think they can change the world, are the ones who do."

Concepts of Obsession

1. When You Give An Excuse or Complain, You are not Obsessed

To make impact you have to stretch and when people give excuses and complain about work, then know that they are not obsessed with what they are doing. Excuses are simply traits of people who are not committed to what they are doing. If you are committed, you will stay in there till you find a way to make it happen.

Thomas Edison was obsessed with making the light bulb work that was why he stayed in there even after series of failures. He kept at it because he was crazy enough to believe that a commercial light bulb is viable and feasible. Obsessed people are all out for it. They burn the bridge. No retreat no surrender. It is what you work that works. If you are not committed to something, you will give up when challenges come or when things get tough.

I would have given up on Engineers Without Borders Nigeria if I was not obsessed with the cause. The organization is just a vehicle to achieve the cause I am obsessed with. There are times when it seems like things will never work, but instead of giving excuses and giving up, I stayed with it. Obsession I believe makes people do remarkable things that others thought was impossible.

2. You are Either Obsessed or Not, No Sitting on the Fence

If you are not obsessed, you are not. No room for half measure. You are either in or you are out. You are either sold out or you are not? When you become obsessed with your objective, you will become equally obsessed with making it work and seeing it succeed. You will always know the person who is obsessed and the one who is not.

If you are not obsessed, you just are not. If your cause or objective has not consumed your thoughts, you will never be obsessed with it. The reason why many people who tried things never succeeded was because they were not obsessed about making it work. They only tried. If they had been obsessed, then they would not have tried. They would have made it work. They certainly would have found a way.

3. Obsession will Never Allow You to Be Average

People obsessed by a cause do more than others do. They give it all they can and more. People who turn out average give average attention to what they do. On the other hand, people who are obsessed give it all they can and extra. Average and obsession are mutually exclusive. There is no way you can be obsessed about something and turn out average.

Grant Cardone said, *"Your obsession is the most valuable tool you have to build the life you deserve and dream of."* If you are not obsessed, you will do the bare minimum to keep going. But once you are obsessed, you will go over and above to make it work. Crazy people do that.

4. If you are obsessed, you will find a way

When people say something is not working, I know they are not obsessed. That's because if one way doesn't work, someone who is obsessed will find the other that works. There is always a way to make your dream a reality, that is why we have a mind. Other animals may not be able to think, but we can.

When you are obsessed about something, you whole being will find a way to make it. You have to be amazed by human ingenuity. It come to play when we are faced with challenges. If you are not obsessed, your mind will not come up with ways to make things work after you have hit a hitch. Obsession challenges the human mental faculty to work.

Steve Jobs was obsessed with making a dent on the universe and making great tools for people that even though Apple was near bankruptcy, everyone predicted that, he was able to find a way to not only keep it from going under but also making it one of the most valuable businesses on earth.

5. Average People Will Criticize and Dissuade You When You Become Obsessed

I have experienced this. You will never get those advice when you are doing things averagely. But become obsessed and people will tell you things to discourage you. Why do they do that? Simply because your obsession exposes their averageness. It's about them not you. They are talking from their experience and the limitation they set on themselves.

Value Givers stay obsessed at all times and get the job done at all cost. They will tell you that you are not the only one. That one should not take life the hard way. They will tell you to take it easy. Only average people take life easy and that is why they remain average. If you want the best out of life, be obsessed and go at it with all you have.

6. Spend Time With Obsessed People and You Will Become Obsessed

John C. Maxwell calls this 'the hot poker principle'. If you put an iron near heat, it will become hot after sometime. If you want to be obsessed, on fire for your cause, get around people who are also on fire. Iron will always sharpen iron. You will always be like the people you associate with.

I had to stop relating with average people when I got to understand this. Association influences you. Obsession is contagious. You will pick it when you associate with people like that. There was a time when I was working for 20 hours a day, then I met someone and he talked me out of it. I was giving my dream all that it took and required then, but he wasn't.

You become like the people you associate with. Or you are like the people you associate with. Associate with people who are obsessed and it will rub on you. Today, I listen to people who are obsessed with what they do. People like Grant Cardone, John C Maxwell and Bishop David Oyedepo challenge my obsession with my cause. The make me increase how obsessed I am.

7. Obsession Means Your Senses Are Alive

When you are obsessed about something, every part of you come alive. Your mind thinks better. That is because obsession is your senses being dominated by your cause. Your mind thinks about it every time. Since your thoughts becomes your feeling and your feeling your action, you will always be acting on whatever consumes your mind.

The mind is amazing. Whatever your mind keeps thinking about, it will come up with multiple ways to achieve it. If you want to do something, just get to consume your mind with it and leave it there. The mind will work on it and give you back the way you need to follow to achieve it.

8. People Obsessed with an idea move the world

When you see people who are making a difference and making history, then you have people who are obsessed with one thing and not many. You don't have to be obsessed with many things at ones. Just be obsessed with one thing and you will be amazed at the impact you are going to make.

You have to be obsessed with one thing and one thing only to shake the world.

9. What You Focus on is What You Become Obsessed With

Whatever you focus on, that is what you are going to become obsessed with. What you focus on feeds your obsession. In Nigeria, we are more focused on making a living and looking rich than on making a difference and living significantly. We focus on the wrong things.

Money is a fruit of a cause. You are to be obsessed with the cause and not the fruit. The fruit will definitely result. Money is never an end on itself rather it's a tool to an end. What you keep focusing on will determine what you become obsessed with.

Becoming Obsessive

I have always been obsessed about one thing or the other since I was a kid. It really is the best way to live life. I can't imagine why other people are not excited about people who are obsessed with making a difference. Our humanity dies when we are not obsessed about making life better for others.

There are things you need to do to become obsessive. In my studies, I discovered there are things obsessive people do. If you imitate them, you will end up becoming them.

1. Tell People About The Impact You Want To Make

Most of us are afraid of telling people what we want to achieve so they don't stop us. My mum tried to brainwash me with that gospel. She said I should not tell people what I want to do. The more she told me that, the more I told everyone. I could not help it. It's like a nature with me to say what I want to do before I even take a step.

If you are a man of integrity, then you will tell people what you want to do and achieve. You see my word is my bond. Once I know it's is something that I should do, I tell people about it then get down to work to find a way to make it happen. If you are not someone who keeps his or her words, you will not be obsessive.

Most of us are afraid of saying it because we know that we will never do what we say. Our words don't mean anything to us.

Someone said that if Joseph, from the Bible, had not told his brothers his dream, he would never have suffered. The reason why he got to the throne was because he told them. Talking about his dream made it part of him. The dream made a way for him.

If he had not told them they won't have been envious and sold him to the Egyptians. And if he hadn't gotten to Egypt, he would never have had the opportunity to serve Potiphar and Pharaoh. He started as a slave and rose to the top. It was obsession with his dream that kept him going.

When you tell people, then you have thrown yourself overboard. That's the way to commit yourself. Throw your heart into it by telling people about it first.

2. Commit Totally To Making A Difference

Obsessive people are committed to whatever they do. Commitment means come rain come shine you will be doing what needs to be done to achieve the results you envision.

If you are not committed to making impact, you will never make it. You will not give it the attention it requires and will never do what needs to be done. You have to stay focused on it.

When you are committed to something you will give it more time. You will never get tired of working there. You will get it done when you commit and have no options. It must work or you will make it work. No room for plan B. Plan B is for people who are not committed and are looking for ways to opt-out if it doesn't work.

Obsessive people have no plan B. If they fail, they fail. If they perish, they perish. They understand that if they have an option from the start, they will never be committed when things get tough. So they burn the boat and the bridge.

3. Be Fully Persuaded That It is Possible to Make Impact

Obsessed people are fully persuaded and convinced that what they are into will make the impact they want to make. Their conviction is evident. If you are not fully and irrevocably convinced about a cause, you will not be obsessed about it. Don't go into anything for the sake of being in something. Go into things because you are persuaded that it's something you need to do.

From experience I have learned that a fully persuaded lamb will make more impact than an unconvinced lion. When you are convinced about something, your eyes becomes single and focused on that one thing. Focus feeds your obsession.

It is not about your size or what you have but how persuaded you are. The reason why people who have nothing start with nothing, create great wealth and make the greatest difference while those with money do nothing. Persuasion and conviction is the difference. If you are persuaded you will give it all that you have and can. To be persuaded means to believe beyond doubt that you can make it happen.

4. Know They Are Responsible For The Impact

People who are not obsessed will tell you that you have done enough. That if you do your enough, then God will do His. What you do is not enough. You are responsible for the results you produce. If you are not producing that result, it means you are not doing enough.

They know that they and only they are responsible for the impact and if they do nothing, they will have nothing. You have to give it what it takes for as long as possible to get what you really want.

That's why obsessed people keep doing things long after others have stopped because they know if impact will be made, it depends on them.

5. Take Massive Action

If your opponent or competitor is obsessed with winning, you are in trouble. Because the person is set to outperform you in every area. It is not about the resources you have at your disposal but how obsessed your are. Obsessed people do more than anyone.

Remember, they are crazy. Crazy people do crazy things. They go where no one will want to go and they do more than others will want to do. They will persist in the action. Even when you are sleeping they will be doing working.

When I wanted to start blogging I thought I cannot do more than a post week. But then I got obsessed and started doing 5 a week. I do 3 now. Don't start anything until you are obsessed. Obsession will make you go above and beyond what is required. You will keep going when others have given up.

You will find time to do whatever you are obsessed about.

6. Be Passionate About What You Do

Obsession is not passion but obsessed people are passionate about what they do. There is no way you will be obsessed about something you are not passionate about. Craziness comes out of being passionate. If people can understand why you do what you do, then you are not passionate about it. You are acting out of your reasoning.

Passion is your emotions coming alive.

7. Be Hungry for More

Don't accept the impact you are making, crave for more. No matter what you have achieved, you can still do more. You should stretch yourself and do more. When you stop being hungry for more, you stop being obsessed.

You know how hungry people do. Don't be satisfied with average. Reach out for more. Always do to beat your best performance.

Is desiring more bad? No it's not., Settling is what is bad. In one of Jesus' parable, he shared about a rich land owner who had a great harvest and decided to settle in and never seek for money. Jesus said his soul was taken. It, therefore, means that we are created to always be hungry. When we stop being hungry, our soul dies or is taken.

Always strive for more. Reach out for more and do more than you are presently doing. If you stop being hungry for more, you are no longer obsessed. Obsession makes you keep reaching high for the best of you.

You keep competing with your best performance. Never rest until you have done more. When you have stretched yourself to do more, stretch yourself further and do more. There is no limit to the expansion of your mind. Like rubber band, it only becomes useful when stretched. You are a living soul, meaning you are only alive when your mind is being stretched and seeking for money.

Keep increasing your focus and your obsession will increase. That is why the obsessed are always learning something new. The more they learn, the hungrier for more they get. They keep striving and reaching out to beat their last performance.

Steve Jobs would have given up and settled in after the success of the iPod. But he became hungry and keep reaching out for more and producing more products that made Apple the most valuable company. He told graduating Stanford University students, "*Stay Hungry. Stay Foolish!*"

He lived hungry and act foolishly because he was obsessed with making a dent on the university. If he were still alive, he would have still been stretching and creating more value for the world. Because there is no end to what can be done. Be obsessed with the value you create and the impact it will have on people and you will always have more value to create for them.

CHAPTER TEN

DEVELOPING A GENEROUS LIFESTYLE

"The value of life is not in its duration, but in its donation. You are not important because of how long you live, you are important because of how effective you live." Dr Myles Munroe.

◆ ◆ ◆

When a newspaper reporter interviewed a farmer, who grew Award-Winning Maize each year, and entered his maize in the Agricultural Show, it was revealed that the farmer shared his seed with his neighbours.

Amazed, the reporter asked, "How can you afford to share your best seed with your neighbours when they are entering their maize in competition with yours each year?"

The farmer smiled knowingly and explained, "The wind picks up pollen from the ripening maize and swirls it from field to field. If my neighbours grow inferior maize, Cross-Pollination will steadily degrade the quality of my maize.

If I am to grow good maize, I must help my neighbours grow a good crop.

So it is with our lives. Those who want to live meaningfully and well, must help enrich the lives of others.

For the value of a life is measured by the lives it touches. And those who choose to be happy, must help others find happiness.

Your greatest achievements will be the one that benefits others. What you do for yourself is called success, while what you do for others is significance.

For the welfare of each is bound up with the welfare of all. If we remove the word giver from Value Giver, all you have left is value. It is the giving that makes the value important not the value itself.

God created the world to operate on generosity. God loves a cheerful giver. Wealth expands when people are generous but shrinks when they are stingy or withhold things.

Economy where money is hoarded shrinks but it expands when people are spending or exchanging money. What is the importance of value when it is not given? It's a waste.

King Solomon talked about this in the Bible. He said,

> "There is one who scatters, yet increases
> more
> And there is one who withholds more than
> is right
> But it leads to poverty.
> The generous soul will be made rich,
> And he who waters will also be watered himself.
> The people will curse him who withholds
> grain,
> But blessing will be on the head of him
> Who sells it."

The world of the generous expands but that of the stingy shrinks. Wealth is created where people are generous. Imagine if all the trees decide not to produce fruits or even release oxygen, humans will be dead in no time.

The best way to kill an economy is not to be generous. If the soil refuses to be generous, humans will die of hunger. Because it will not produce any crop.

Poor nations like Nigeria are places where people hoard value rather than give it. Those who get the most out of life are the ones who give the most. I have made progress more by being generous with value than hoarding. The Nigerian economy is built on being stingy not being generous. Just take a sampling of nations and you will find out that nations that are generous are the richest, while those who are not are poor nations.

All poor nations need to do is to change their mentality and begin to create value and give to other nations. The world of the generous nation expands because opportunities open up to those nations.

Value Givers are generous with values

I started my writing career by giving out books for free. I wrote more than a 100 books and gave them away free of charge. A friend told me to withdraw all the books I have given and stopped giving them out for free. I continued. The booked helped many and made a difference in their lives. Those books made me a consultant and coach too. I continue to reap harvest from them. Giving has always made a way for me. It is not easy giving but it is the best way to make progress.

To be a value giver, you have to live by your generosity. Generosity is the quality of being kind and understanding, the willingness to give others things that have value.

For Nigeria to become a great nation we have to be people who give value to others. To give value is to serve people. Jesus said, "The greatest is the one who serves."

A guy wanted to join our book writing course. He asked for discount and I gave him 25% discount. He insisted he wanted 50%. I told him I cannot go lower than that. Instead I will teach him for free and that was what I did. We start living when we start giving value to people.

In 2001, the author Stephen King gave a commencement address to graduating students of Vassar College in the US. He said the following among other things:

Giving isn't about the receiver or the gift but the giver. It's for the giver. One doesn't open one's wallet to improve the world, although it's nice when that happens. One opens one's wallet to improve one's self. I give because it's the only concrete way I have of saying I'm glad to be alive and that I can earn my daily bread doing what I love. I hope you will be similarly grateful to be alive and that you will also be glad to do whatever it is you wind up doing.... Giving is a way of taking the focus off the money we make and putting it back where it belongs - on the lives we lead, the families we raise, and the communities that nurture us.

So I ask you to begin the next great phase of your life by giving, and to continue as you begin. I think you'll find that in the end you get far more than you ever had and do more good than you ever dreamed."

Generous makes your world bigger than you can ever dream of it to be.

There are two types of people:

1. Value Givers
2. Value Takers

.Value Givers create and give value, while Value Takers don't create but only take. Value takers look for places where others have created value already and become part of it. Their goal is just to consume what has already been done. They are consumers and not creators.

Value givers are the people who move society forward while value takers stagnates it and take it back a thousand years or even cause it's extinction. By not creating value, they are destroying value. Why is it that most businesses in Nigeria are failing? It is populated with value takers. They destroy the value that has been created. Wealth is created by value giver. Value Givers advance the world while Value Takers shrinks the world.

I want the world I live in to continually expand. That is why I chose to live by my generosity.

Takers Make a Nation Poor

Adam Grant said, "*Takers are self-serving in their interactions. It's all about what can you do for me.*" There is a direct correlation between how poor a nation is and the number of takers within it. A nation with a low standard of living, where more people are living below the poverty line, is one that is filled with people who are waiting to take value rather than create it. Takers impoverish a nation.

On the other hand, a nation with givers who create wealth will grow and experience prosperity. The greater the number of people who are givers in a nation, the greater the opportunities and benefits that flows to everyone. Givers create value and serve people. They understand that opportunities they desire are created by providing something of value to people.

People who do nothing and expect that someone will give them a job or money are the kind of people who impoverish a nation. Everyone of us exist to contribute something to the nation where we are. We are to live by our generosity or contribution and not by what we get. Unfortunately, most people think that their lives are measured by what they get.

That is the major challenge in poor nations like Nigeria. Everyone believes that society will celebrate them for what they have and not what they contribute to it. As such we are constantly taking from the nation without creating anything in return. Nigeria is poor because we are a nation of takers. Jesus said, *"Take heed and beware of covetousness, for one's life does not consist in the abundance of the things he possess."* A nation become great when its citizens begin to make contribution to its wealth and not take from it.

Take Dubai for instance, they have a giver mindset. They used the revenue they had to create more wealth than the needed. Since they maintained that mindset, they are continually creating wealth. I believe they followed the Advice Paul gave his protege, Timothy, when he wrote, *"Command those who are rich in this present age not to be haughty, nor to trust in uncertain riches but in the living God, who gives us richly all things to enjoy. Let them do good, that they be rich in good works, ready to give, willing to share, storing up for themselves a good foundation for the time to come..."* Dubai is a nation of givers.

If all you do is receive your salary without using it to increase the contributions you make, you are simply a taker. All takers do is to milk the cow dry. They don't even bother to feed the cow. They don't care if the cow dies of hunger as long as it can produce some milk for them. Givers on the other hand will invest more in the cow than they take from it as an investment in the future production of the cow. From what they get from the one cow, they will own a ranch and then diversify their income streams.

Things You Need To Know About Generosity
1. People with abundance mindset are generous. People who are not generous believe more in scarcity than abundance. If you have abundance mindset, you will easily give.
2. You can only give what you have. What you give is what you have. Whatever you keep owns you, while what you give is what you have control over. You can never give what you don't have, can you?
3. Generosity is proof that you believe in yourself. People who do not give don't believe in themselves. If you really believe in yourself and see value in yourself, you will not keep things from people. You will create and give them value.
4. Whatever you hold on to diminish in value. Something only become valuable when it is shared with others. Value is with the receiver not the person who has it. A seed has no value until it is given to the soil.
5. Generosity is the path to great riches and abundance. Only in Nigeria will you find people who became billionaires without first being generous. They became rich by taking and not by giving. But giving starts the receiving process. Real wealth is created when value is given.
6. Your life is a measure of your giving. Life is not measured by what you take and accumulate but what you give. If all you have been doing is taking or receiving without giving, then you are not living. Every living thing should give.
7. What you give enriches other, what you take enriches you. There is no way you can enrich others without enriching yourself. What you take only benefits you and deprives others, but what you give benefits you and others.
8. Giving starts the receiving process. If you want to receive, first give. The more you give, the more doors you open for yourself.
I sent my books to pastors, then, a journalist entered one of the pastors office and saw my book. He picked my number and called me and then published what I wrote in a national newspaper. If I haven't given, I won't have received.

9. Generosity is the only proof that you are alive. If you are alive, you will give to others. If you are not giving, you are dead.

10. The more you give, the more you have. Generosity works and opens doors. The less you give, the less you have. Massive giving results in massive return. Bill Gates decided to give his wealth, instead of becoming just another billionaire, he still maintained his place as one of the richest people on earth.

A few years back, while teaching the Public Servants in Ondo State, Nigeria, I went beyond their expectations and gave them free handouts and books. That opened the door for me to be a consultant earning 6 figure income even when I knew nothing about being a consultant.

Giving works!

Most times people take generous people to be soft, easy, fool and pushovers. I have had a lot of experience with takers.

My soul is oppressed each time I experience takers. I can't imagine people who just position themselves to take and never to give. What are they expecting from life? How can they be happy and fulfilled without giving?

This made me want to know the reason why people don't really want to give but just to take. Many have made taking a lifestyle.

Why People Don't Give

1. Fear

They are afraid that if they give, they will lack and will be taken for granted. Yes fear has turned many people into takers with a narrow life.

I was not taught to give. My dad modeled giving to me. Most people were modeled stinginess. So the fear of not having makes many people to hide and keep the little they have. And of course, it remains little. It only grows when it is shared.

2. Scarcity Mentality

A lot of people just don't give because they see scarcity in everything. They believe that if they give value to others, they will have nothing else remaining. I have found that not to be true. The more I give, the more I have. Giving open you to the world of abundance.

Do I need that guys money. Yes of course. But I was told never to be desperate when I am in need. In need, I should be a giver not a taker. I should come with my skills ready to help people and not just present my needs.

Who To Give To

1. Give to those in need

It's not all needs that you can use your skills to provide value for. There is no want of people who have needs you can meet. They are all out there. If you want your needs meet, then you need to learn to prioritize giving people value that meets their needs.

2. People who help you meet your needs or solve your problems

If a product meets your needs, find a way to give to the person or company. Give them by doing more business with them. You can also give to them by telling others about the company and their products or helping them to get more sales. You can also give them ideas on how to improve their value.

3. People who pour their wisdom into you

Don't take anything for granted. If they give you for free, give back. It cost them to get it. When I read an article by some and it helped me, the next thing I will do is to buy up the books the person has written and even consider being part of their program.

I have a mentor. I wanted him to mentor me and he said its $5000, I said no problem. I don't have the money then. So I started buying everything he produces. I paid him that way and tell people about him. I have all the books he has written. I paid him that way and he mentored me indirectly and still does.

Develop Generous Lifestyle

1. Give Something Beneficial to People

Whatever you know will benefit someone, you can get it for the person. This is why I hardly make friends. Because if you are my friend and I read a good book and know that it will help you, I buy it for you. Money will never last forever. So if you want to have your needs met, give people what you know will benefit them.

That's what I do. I find what will benefit you, and get it to you. Keep getting to know what people need and supplying it to them.

2. Give More Than You Get

If you only give what you receive then you are not generous. Generous people give because they have and know that it is good to give. It is natural to give and it's beneficial too.

Here are benefits of giving

- Reduce stress
- Increase happiness
- Supports health
- Enhance sense of purpose
- Fights depression
- Increase lifespan

When King Solomon said vanity is vanity, all he could have done was become more generous and things will change. He became a taker and his vision narrowed. He was more focused on himself and what he can get. He became frustrated and unfulfilled.

I buy books to say thank you to the person who took time to share his wisdom with me. He is generous to me so I give him back in generosity too. Do you know how many people hoard their wisdoms and go to the grave with them? When a person dies, a generation of wisdom is lost forever.

Always meet people with generosity. This is a lifestyle that can be developed and is developed over time.

3. Give What People Values

Don't just give anything, give what the other person values. You will have to know what the person values and then deliver it to them.

If you give to someone what they don't value you really are not generous. If you know that someone needs food to eat and you give the person a new car, you are not being generous. It's not about the amount you gave but how valuable it is to the person. You should have given the person a car and food too. It's the food that the person values.

4. Persist in Giving

There is this saying that you should not grow weary in giving, for you will reap in due season. When you start giving, you may not even see any return benefit to you. That doesn't mean you should stop giving. Persist in giving and you will break the glass ceiling and reap enormous benefits of your generosity.

I love how Solomon said it. He said, *"He who observes the wind will not sow (give), and he who regards the clouds will not reap. In the morning sow your seed, and in the evening do not withhold your hand; for you do not know which will prosper,, either this or that. Or whether both alike will be good."* Just make sure that you keep adding value to people. Even if you have done it a 100 times and you don't see results, keep doing it more and don't give up.

Keep creating and giving value. Be relentless. You never know the one that will work for you. Persist in giving value. Don't get discouraged. Your reap if you faint not.

About The Author

Oladimeji Olutimehin is a high impact social entrepreneur, author, coach and consultant. He is the founder of Engineer Without Borders Nigeria and First Millionaire Maker Nig. Ltd and co-founder of MegaGrowth Solutions Ltd. He is a recognized authority in creating personal as well as business value.

He is the author of several books, including The Millionaire Maker, Secrets of the Millionaire Employee Mindset, and One Minute Millionaire Employee. Dimeji is also a regular blogger.

Dimeji's expertise is based on his real-real-world experience of training people, studying people, consulting and creating values. He founded Engineers Without Borders Nigeria in the university to meet the gap created by lack of real-life experience in university education and 1st Millionaire Maker Nig. Ltd to help people grow to be all they as well as to live a fulfilled life.

Dimeji is an Electrical/Electronics Engineering graduate of the Federal University of Technology in Yola and has served on the board of Engineers Without Borders International based in Washington DC, USA. He loves reading, writing, traveling, meeting new people, developing people and watching movies. He lives in Akure, Ondo State, Nigeria.

To get him to bring his Value Giver program to your organization, you can contact him through:

Website: www.1stmillionairemaker.com
Blog: www.1stmillionairemaker.com/blog
email: 1stmillionairemakerng@gmail.com
Call/WhatsApp: +2349071602727
personal email: thelordsearth@yahoo.com